BOOK OF MEMORIES AND A HISTORY OF
HOPEWELL UNITED METHODIST CHURCH

ESTELLE VINSON ALLEN;
ANNETTE ALLEN EDWARDS

WESTBOW
PRESS®
A DIVISION OF THOMAS NELSON
& ZONDERVAN

WestBow Press books may be ordered through booksellers or by contacting:

WestBow Press
A Division of Thomas Nelson & Zondervan
1663 Liberty Drive
Bloomington, IN 47403
www.westbowpress.com
1 (866) 928-1240

ISBN: 978-1-9736-1155-4 (sc)
ISBN: 978-1-9736-1976-5 (hc)

Print information available on the last page.

WestBow Press rev. date: 02/24/2018

Dedication

This book is lovingly dedicated to the memory of:
Leon Hartwell Allen, Sr. (1911-1985)
Husband of

Estelle Vinson Allen (1909-2010)

Estelle Allen and Leon Allen, mid 1970's

Acknowledgements

Acknowledgement is given to all who responded to my mother's requests for their memories to be included in this book. My sincere thanks to each person who contributed and a special thank you goes to Faith Hoople for typing up many of the memories for her. Thanks to Alicia Spado for her contribution and to her and Carol Story for their proofreading and editing expertise.

Accolades to Ken and Carol Story for contributing the section on the Hopewell Cemetery!

Above picture: Estelle Vinson Allen on left, Annette Allen Edwards on right.

Foreword

The procrastinator that I am, I take pen in hand to get this book put together. Well, that is not exactly right. Truth is that my mother, Estelle Vinson Allen, took pen in hand and wrote most of this material. I am simply trying to combine it and make a printed edition of all her notes, memories, and the material she accumulated during the last few years of her life. I start by mentioning that this idea came to her in 1995, soon after the completion of her book "We Remember The Best" about her mother, Laura Olivia Story Vinson, in 1994. I promised to help her get the book written and published. It seemed I was always "too busy" or thought I was too busy, to get started on the project.

At any rate, for a long time, nothing more was done. When she passed in 2010, I grieved over my losses and continued to procrastinate. Yes, I felt guilty, but just not guilty enough to get started. It is now over 6 years since her death and this must be completed. Perhaps I will complete this project some 20-plus years after its conception.

I am sure it was Mama's desire to have as much input from others as they would give for this book. I feel that my brother, Leon Hartwell Allen, Jr., did a wonderful job when writing his memories, so much so that he probably should have been the one to spearhead this production!

The following page will serve as a brief introduction to my mother.

Annette Allen Edwards
May, 2015
(Modified February, 2017)

Elizabeth Estelle Vinson Allen

Her parents were Marcellus Neal (Dock) and Laura Olivia Story Vinson.

She was born August 31, 1909, in Tallapoosa County, AL.

The family moved to "Floyd Place" on Marvyn Road (Hwy 51) in Lee County in 1910. They moved about often, as her father was a sharecropper.

She joined Hopewell Methodist Protestant Church (now Hopewell United Methodist Church) at 9 years of age in 1918. This church has been very important to her all her life. She was involved in the reorganization of the Christian Endeavor for youth and the first Women's Society of Christian Service missionary group for the women of the church.

Her great grandparents, James and Ellender Duke Story, were charter members of the Hopewell Methodist Protestant Church. Her grandfather and step grandmother, Judge Aaron and Sultana Cadenhead Story, deeded the property to the church in 1900.

She lived for 2 years (1917-1919) in Salem on the farm of her great Uncle "Buck" Jones. Buck was sheriff of Lee County who was killed in the line of duty. The present Lee County administrative building/jail is dedicated in his memory.

She attended Clift High School in Opelika and Troy State Teachers College in Troy, AL.

She taught school in the Salem and Smith's Station elementary schools in early 1930's.

She married Leon Hartwell Allen, Sr., son of John Leland and Emma Irene Jones Allen in 1935. They had three children: Dr. L. H. Allen, Jr., Annette A. Edwards, and Dr. Lenora Allen.

She was an active PTA parent at Beauregard School and in the Lee County PTA. (Parent Teachers Association)

She worked as a federal employee in the Agricultural Stabilization and Conservation Service office at the Lee County courthouse for over 25 years.

Hopewell U. M. C.

Preface

In 1995, while recuperating in a nursing home, there came into my heart a longing to leave some kind of tribute to Hopewell Methodist Church. It has been a home church to me and to so many of my ancestors and friends. Hopewell has always been an important part of my life.

So, in 1996, I mailed a request to many people to send their memories of Hopewell. I received very few responses. In 1997, I mailed a letter to all I could think of and had addresses for.

This book contains responses from those that were inspired to write and send me their memories. I am very thankful for those who did and thereby made this book better. It was a disappointment that more people did not respond.

Please note that in the sections about my memories of the men and women of Hopewell, I apologize up front if I have left someone out. Most people are included as they came to my mind.

Estelle Vinson Allen

Contents

Hopewell Church

Hopewell Methodist Protestant Church 1846 – 1939
Hopewell Methodist Church 1939 – 1968
Hopewell United Methodist Church 1968 – present

Hopewell Church was established in the mid to late 1840's as Hopewell Methodist Protestant Church. The year accepted by most people is 1846. We have a 1929 Catechism for Beginners for the Methodist Protestant Church, although it is not in the best of shape now.

In 1939, the three major Methodist Churches (Methodist Protestant, Methodist Episcopal, and Methodist Episcopal, South) joined together to become The Methodist Church. The Methodist Church united with Evangelical United Brethren Church in 1968 to become The United Methodist Church.

The Methodist Protestant Denomination was started in Alabama in 1829. The earliest microfilm minutes are of the 1846 Alabama Conference. These records are in the History and Archives Department in Montgomery, Alabama. The 1849 minutes show the Jefferson Circuit was divided and the Russell County Circuit was formed with four churches, Hopewell being one of them. Minutes of the 1852 Methodist Protestant Conference held at Robinson Springs Church show Rev. John O. E. Cowart as pastor of the Russell County Circuit. Minutes of the 1871 conference show W. C. Jones was the Layman and Rev. A. H. Ledbetter was pastor. The Lee Circuit, consisting of five churches (Hopewell, Pierce Chapel, Morris Chapel, Pine Grove and Beulah), was formed in 1876.

Some family records during this period are those of James Story. He married his third wife, Ellender Duke in 1836 and brought his bride from Harris County, GA to a log house about ¾ mile west of Hopewell's current site. Another reference to the beginning of Hopewell Methodist Protestant Church is the obituary of Ellender Duke Story (10/20/1809 - 1/7/1901), which states that James and Ellender Story were charter members of Hopewell Methodist Protestant Church.

The Census Records of 1840 indicate that James Story lived in the same Township (No. 18) as the deed shows the location of the church building. James Story, born in 1794 in Oglethorpe County, GA, died January, 1859, in Russell County, AL (now Lee County) and was buried in Hopewell Church Cemetery in January, 1859. This is the earliest recorded burial in the Land.

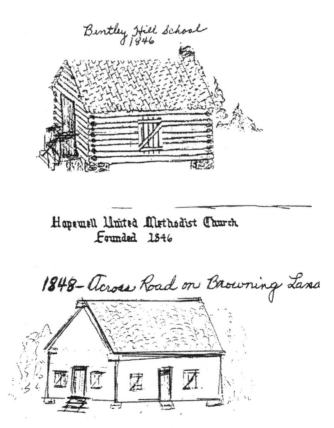

Bentley Hill School
1846

Hopewell United Methodist Church
Founded 1846

1848— Across Road on Browning Lane

(Early meeting buildings)

Oral tradition is that in the beginning, meetings were held in a small log school house on land owned by a Mr. Bentley. The first building was a rough frame weather-boarded hull with wooden shutters. Blocks were nailed to the walls and tallow candles put on them for light. There were no musical instruments. The preacher or song leader would read the song through, and then read two lines. Everyone would sing those two lines and continue this process until the song was finished. The song book was "Prayer and Praise" and written in tunes long, short, or common meter.

Large crowds came to meetings at Hopewell. One night, during a Revival in 1880, the southwest corner of the church collapsed. This was repaired right away. In 1898, the church was remodeled and made longer. For a time, men sat on one side of the church and the women on the other side.

In 1907, while Rev. C. W. Walton was pastor, an organ was purchased. Miss Sammie Ramsey was the organist. In 1925, a larger church was built while Rev. W. A. Lynch was pastor. In 1930, a piano was bought and Miss Mildred Story was the pianist. In 1952, Sunday School rooms were completed on the north of the church. In 1963, more rooms were added on the south side of the church, including the 'old fellowship hall'. In 1984, a steeple was erected. In 1989, the cross was erected in the cemetery in memory of Evanelle Story Porch. Circuit-wide Easter Sunrise Services are held near the cross. A new Fellowship Hall was built in 1999 and was dedicated July 25, 1999.

The first youth organization recorded was the "Christian Endeavor" organized in 1897 by Miss Arie Lynch. In 1931, Rev. A. L. Lumpkin helped reorganize The Christian Endeavor at Hopewell. It remained active until after 1940 when it became known as MYF (Methodist Youth Fellowship). Later it became known as UMYF (United Methodist Youth Fellowship).

According to memos of Mrs. Ollie Story Vinson, the first Sunday School teacher she recalled was Miss Esther Lynch and the first Sunday School superintendent was Mr. George E. Vinson, about 1890. For some time, Sunday School was not held in the winter months because there was no form of heat in the open church. Later, after a stove was installed and the building improved, Sunday School was held on a more regular basis.

The first Missionary Society (women's group) was organized in 1931 under the leadership of Rev. A. L. Lumpkin, with Miss Estelle Vinson as president. On September 7, 1940, after unification, the Charter meeting of the Women's Society of Christian Service was held. Rev. Wilbur Walton, pastor, conducted the service. Mrs. Jesse Story was elected president. The organization is known today *(1998)* as The United Methodist Women. The 50th Anniversary of Hopewell UMW was held June 13, 1981. Mrs. Barbara Vinson Chandler was elected president in 1996. (When this book was printed, Hopewell no longer had a United Methodist Women's group. The women's group call themselves Christian Women's Fellowship now.)

Some family names of the Hopewell Community from the 1840 and 1850 Censuses were, Bentley, Browning, Hopkins, Jackson, Johnson, Jones, Lynch, Martin, McConnell, Riddle, Ramsey and Story. Descendants of some of these families still attend services at Hopewell.

Many Methodist ministers grew up as members of Hopewell or were of the Hopewell heritage. Included in their number are Rev. W.H. Lynch, Rev. Bentley, Rev. Judge Aaron Story, Rev. Cooper Martin, Rev. Seaborn Jones, Rev. Andrew Jones, Rev. S. H. (Kim) Lynch, Rev. W. O. Lynch, Sr., Rev. W. O. Lynch, Jr., Rev. Gladys Lynch, Rev. Jack Lynch, Rev. Arthur Lynch, Rev. Hershall Lynch, and Rev. G.L. Story, Jr. Daniel Frank (Doc) Story was a licensed Methodist Protestant Exhorter (1870 until his death in 1885).

In previous years, singings were often held at Hopewell as it was known as the "singing and shouting" church. In 1957, a Homecoming was held with a large attendance. On June 22, 1986, the 140th Anniversary of Hopewell was celebrated with a Homecoming. The 150th Anniversary was celebrated on June 23, 1996, the 160th on July 16, 2006, and on June 26, 2016, the 170th Anniversary was celebrated.

Current record of deed of Hopewell United Methodist Church property is on file in the Lee County Courthouse, Opelika, AL. Book Reference

42, pages 298-299, in Range 27, Township 18, Section 26. The property was deeded in 1900 by Mr. & Mrs. J. A. Story. Judge A. Story bought the property from Mr. Browning in 1888. No previous deed has been located when the church was first built in 1848.

Estelle Vinson Allen, Historian (2006)

****

The Hopewell Cemetery Association was formed as a result of the church having deeded land to them in December, 2009. The Church established a library in 2014. In 2015, renovations to the Sanctuary began, which included new heat and air units, resurfaced hardwood floors, new carpet, new front doors, and painting. In June, 2015, the road was paved through the Hopewell Cemetery and around the church. "The History Corner" was created in part of the old fellowship hall in 2016. During the 170th Anniversary, it was dedicated in remembrance of Estelle Vinson Allen.

Alicia Estelle Childress Spado, Historian (2016)

History Corner dedicated to Estelle V. Allen

The Old Church – Fact & Fiction

"For where two or three are gathered together in my name, there am I in the midst of them." Matthew 18:20 KJV

Since I don't remember the old church very well, I'll call my description a story with some truth.

I remember my mother saying that she had heard people say a small group first met in Bentley School House which was on the hill just southwest of our present church. At our Homecoming in 1986, an older person told me that she had heard the group built a brush arbor to meet in before they built a building. Both accounts could be correct. She also told me that someone in the group said, "We hope to do well in the sight of the Lord," and that is how the church came to be named Hopewell.

When the first church building was built, I expect the material came from the virgin forest of long leaf pine. The trees were probably given by some plantation owner who might have had a mill to make the trees into lumber. It could have been Mr. Browning.

Probably after crop lay-by time, the men and young boys gathered together and united their skills in raising this building to be dedicated to the worship of God. It was a small weather boarded building, but I know they praised the Lord when it was finished.

The sketch of the outside of the old building is mostly imagination. I was old enough when the new church was finished in 1925 to remember more details. It's like when we travel the same road every day and never see the flowers.

I remember more about the inside. The pews were wide plank seats and had about a six inch plank at the top. So there was a wide open area behind you and no support for your back. (Maybe that is why so many knelt to pray; they could rest their backs!) I remember kneeling beside my mother, not having my eyes closed, and peeping through the pews at the people behind us. There was the "amen" corner off to the side of the pulpit area; and you often heard an "amen" from the men who sat there when the preacher said some likeable thing. There were several small lamps on shelves around the church. They were about five feet high. Behind each lamp was some type of reflector. I remember a piece of furniture like a chest about four feet long in one corner from which a man would get some materials to use at the Saturday business meeting.

I also remember a shelf that held a water bucket and a dipper. My brother does not remember these two things, but he remembers a lamp hanging over the pulpit and a big heater in the upper center of the sanctuary.

Going to church when I was young was an event that took several hours. You went by horse and buggy, mule and wagon, horseback or walked. Those who have never experienced riding to church in a buggy or wagon and hearing the sound of the wheels grinding in the ruts of pine woods, on the sandy road have missed an indescribable sound.

Now, water is piped in, but in the old days, we got our water from a spring down the hill and later a well in the front yard.

Our lights were a lightwood torch, candles, and small oil lamps. Our physical lights have changed to nice electric fixtures, but His Light never changes.

"I am the Light of the World." John 8:12 (KJV)

I have witnessed many people joining the church at Hopewell during my lifetime. Many have become good leaders in many other places. Leon and

I witnessed our three children joining Hopewell following the example of many before them. We rejoiced and were happy in their decisions. There are three others that so impressed me when they joined the church that I want to mention them as well. Richard McConnell joined while Rev. Bob Wilson was pastor. Debra Foster (Causey) joined while Rev. Robert Warren was pastor. Debra had helped me in Sunday School and Bible School. She was so pleasant and helpful that it was easy to love her. Some of us were attending services at Pierce Chapel Church one night when Carolyn Barker (McConnell) joined there.

Estelle Vinson Allen

Historical Remarks by Mrs. Leon Allen

I, too, welcome you to Homecoming today at Hopewell on our 140th anniversary—June 22, 1986.

I read recently this thought, "The present is the only time we have for the learnings of the past to be whispered into the ear of the future for continued action." May that be our aim today.

We've come up with a date of 1846 for the starting of Hopewell Methodist Protestant Church. Available minutes of the 1846 Conference show Mt. Jefferson with 8 churches. The 1849 minutes indicate that Mt. Jefferson Circuit was divided and Russell County Circuit was started with four churches from the Mt. Jefferson Circuit. The date may not "hit the nail on the head," but it is near. When Auburn, Alabama, celebrated its 150th Anniversary this year, some said it was three years early: that the Mayor wanted to celebrate it during election year. (I had to add a bit of political flavor.)

The only other Homecoming I can remember having at Hopewell was in 1957. I have a copy of that bulletin. My mother, Mrs. Ollie Story Vinson, gave the history. Rev. Charles Pittman was pastor. Rev. Glenn Sirmon preached the morning sermon and Rev. A. L. Lumpkin preached in the afternoon. In the announcements, Rev. Bob Wilson was to preach at the revival in August.

Originally, I had intended to read what I wrote on the history of Hopewell, but I found a 1935 copy of the Alabama Conference Journal of the Methodist Protestant Church that my mother had. There were so many things in it we could relate to, that I decided to tell a few facts from it.

Some of us are old enough to remember 1935. That is the year that I got married. I do remember that!

This 107th session of the Methodist Protestant Church in Alabama was held November 6, 7, and 8, 1935, at Antioch church on Macon Circuit, near Notasulga, Alabama. Dr. J. S. Eddins was President, Rev. T. C. Casaday, Secretary.

The first day's program included: morning sermon by Rev. Hershall Lynch. (We always thought he was someone very special for he had been a missionary). Rev. C. W. Walton led the morning prayer. W. H. Bentley gave the history of Antioch's 100th anniversary, established in 1835. Rev. P A. Lynch was pastor of Macon Circuit.

Talks were given on church union. A visitor, Dr. O V. Calhoun, Presiding Elder of the Montgomery District of the Methodist Episcopal Church, South, told of the common heritage of all Methodism. Another visitor, Dr. W. F. Calhoun, Pastor of Dexter Avenue Methodist Episcopal Church, South, had a message on the strong desire to see plans of union for the three major Methodist churches become a reality.

Dr. J. S. Eddins, President, Alabama Methodist Protestant Conference, continued the talks by saying this: "If a United Methodism does become a reality in God's own time, and in God's own way, our church need not be so concerned about what it may get out of the Union, but what we will bring into it. If our Methodist Protestant Church has done nothing more, through its struggles, than to open the doors of all conferences of Methodism to lay people, giving to them both a voice and a vote in the Council of the Church, she has justified her claim to be born of God and to have lived gloriously for the Lord's sake."

Some other facts gleaned: Wilbur Walton was recommended to be suitable for a loan of $50. He was in school in High Point, N. C. Others who received loans included: Hershall Lynch, Otis Lynch, and Gladys Lynch. Balance in the Education Fund was $20.00.

Dr. J. Bibb Mills, Supt. Anti-Saloon, addressed the conference. An offering was taken in the amount of $17.89 for this work. Rev. Otis Lynch asked to be released from the Union Circuit and to be transferred to the Arkansas Conference.

In 1935, Lee Circuit had 5 churches, 499 members, promised to pay pastor $645.00, paid the pastor $482; due $163. Of that, Hopewell promised $175, paid $126; due $49.00 as of November 1, 1935. Value of the churches was $4200.00. (This was 50-1/2 years ago!) Rev. A. E. Maddox was Pastor of Lee Circuit.

Some of those listed in the roll of the dead in this Journal were: Peyton Bibb, L. R. Mills, J. F. Bentley (1859), W. M. Bentley (1863), L. L. Hill, J. L. Mosley, A. H. Ledbetter, T. J. Ledbetter, S. H. (Kim) Lynch (1921), Mrs. Emma Ray. *{I believe the dates in parentheses are the years of death.}*

Mama's talk continues...We regret that because of health problems, Dr. Wilbur Walton could not be with us today

I would like to mention a few things about Wilbur's father, Rev. C. W. Walton. He served Lee Circuit in 1906-07 and in 1919-22, for a total of 5 years. Brother Charlie was a very dramatic and forceful preacher. He could have been a comedian, but he answered the Lord's Call for him to preach the gospel instead. He had a very loving wife that he called "Miss Laura" in his sometimes drawling voice. He often told some joke on her in his winsome, dry wit way. Bro. Walton was President of the Alabama Methodist Protestant Conference for four years.

Now, something about Wilbur. He was licensed to preach at Union Methodist Protestant Church on the Macon Circuit. He had a great heritage and example to follow. He was in school in High Point, N.C. in 1935. In 1936, he was appointed to Lee Circuit and came bringing his lovely and adroit wife, Annie Ledbetter Walton. Wilbur served the Lee Circuit for five consecutive years, more than any other. During those five years, 33 people joined Hopewell Church. Unification came in 1939 and became a reality in 1940. Wilbur and Annie have two children, Ann Judson and Wilbur, Jr.

Rev. Wilbur Walton was ordained Deacon in 1936 and Elder in 1938. He served as a U. S. Army Chaplain from 1943 to 1946. In 1939, he received his B. S. Degree from Auburn and a D.D. Degree from Birmingham Southern in 1952.

Again, I'd like to say that we regret Wilbur could not come today. He sent a testimony, which I will read at this time.

Testimony of Dr. Wilbur Walton

Prepared for Hopewell UM Church Homecoming, June 22, 1986
Read by Estelle Vinson Allen (morning)

It has been a long time since I was pastor of the Lee Circuit. Of course, it was my first pastorate, and I had everything to learn. I can truly say that the five years I served the Lee Circuit, as it was composed at that time, were the most meaningful times of my entire ministry. I have been fortunate to serve three different times as District Superintendent, and have served as pastor of some great churches, such as First Church Dothan and First Church Montgomery, but always think of the Lee Circuit as being home.

I remember the time I preached at the first Sunday I served as pastor, Mr. Jesse Story and I were down at a spring of cold clear water for a refreshing drink, and just as we started to leave to go back to the church, he reached in his pocket and came out with a few bills and some change. He held the money out to me and I asked him what it was. He said, "This is for you---it is to go on your salary." I was surprised and hesitated to take the money. However, he insisted and I finally took it with this observation,

"Well, I am not worth it; but someday I am going to be worth it!" I hope I have been worth something during these many years I have sought to serve Christ and His church. *Mama's note (If I remember, it was $3.60. I've heard the story several times.)*

I remember on one occasion when I was preaching with plenty of fervor and knocked my watch off the pulpit. As it fell to the floor I reached over to pick it up and said "It won't hurt it." As I started to continue with the sermon, I shouted out in a loud voice, "IT WON'T HURT IT!"

There were many times when something happened to keep members of the congregation awake! However, I will truthfully say that my greatest thrill was to see a number of people come down the aisle and commit themselves to Christ and His church.

Introduction of Rev. W. O. Lynch, Jr.

June 22, 1986 (morning)
Rev. W. O. Lynch, Jr. from the Louisiana Conference, with an appointment in New Orleans, will bring our morning message.

I doubt if there is another Methodist minister in the world with more "preacher" relatives than W. O. Lynch, Jr. He has a great heritage. His father, Rev. W. O. Lynch, Sr., was licensed to preach in 1931. His grandfather, Rev. S. H. "Kim" Lynch, was converted early in life and joined Hopewell Methodist Protestant Church. He was licensed to preach in 1901 and ordained in 1905. He served several churches including Lee Circuit. He was President of the Alabama Methodist Protestant Conference in 1916 and 1917, and was a delegate to General Conference. He married Nora Louise Jones and they had four children. One of those is here today, Mrs. Thelma Lynch Williams from West Virginia. Rev. S. H. "Kim" Lynch died in 1921 after a short, but full life.

Some other "relative" ministers of W. O., Jr. are: Rev. W. A. Lynch, brother, Revs. Andrew and Seaborn Jones, brothers-in-law, Rev. Hershall Lynch, cousin, and Rev. Gladys Lynch, uncle; also, some Bentleys, Storys, Jacksons and probably more. Those known living are: Rev. Jack Lynch, Virginia Conference and Dr. G. L. Story, Jr., of Illinois.

His wife, mother and a brother are here today, as well as other family members. We welcome all of you.

W. O., we are so happy for you to be here today to bring our morning message.

Brief Comments Sent to Homecoming by Some of our Former Pastors

Read by EVA
June 22, 1986 (afternoon)

1. Rev. Wilbur Walton – (I read his testimony this morning.)
2. Rev. Bob Wilson—(afternoon speaker)
3. Rev. T. H Maxey sends regrets that because of a previous appointment, he could not come. He does remember how lovingly Lee Circuit received him and his wife, Bobbie, when they came as a young couple.
4. Rev. Glenn Sirmon said "The people of Hopewell gave him a good feeling about being a Methodist pastor."
5. Rev. James Love said he has a 1954 bulletin that shows Hopewell started sending resident members the Alabama Christian Advocate at $1.13 each annual subscription. (It is now $7.50)
6. Rev. Gillis Crenshaw remembers the unique wholeness between all age groups at Hopewell.
7. Rev. R. C. Warren said, "When I drove up to Hopewell Church, I knew my call to the ministry was true."
8. Rev. Sam Lowery was on Lee Circuit for only 9 months, but remembers the people were strongly tied together.

9. Rev. Bobby Holladay said the three years he spent on Lee Circuit were three of his most enjoyable years. He also said, "You gave me and my family love, support and encouragement. I'll always remember the beauty of Hopewell Church."

10. Rev. C. D. Monday said that we were his first full time charge and he was welcomed with love, kindness and helpfulness. He remembers having the air conditioner installed while he was here.

11. Rev. Robert Warren especially remembers two things, gladness over the conversion of Debra Foster and sadness over the disappearance of Mrs. Ruth Dorsey.

12. Rev. Eugene Hall sends best wishes for a good day. He has church responsibilities and could not come.

My Testimony

Estelle Vinson Allen
June 22, 1986 (afternoon)

Hopewell is a sacred place to me. My great grandparents, James and Ellen Duke Story, were Charter members at Hopewell. My grandparents, Judge Aaron and Laura Jane Thomas Story, my parents, Dock and Ollie Story Vinson and my husband, Leon H. Allen, Sr. were all faithful and devoted members of this church. Also, many other relatives and friends found and served the LORD from this hilltop church.

I joined Hopewell Church in July, 1918, under the powerful preaching of Rev. Kim Lynch. I was young. That is not so much the custom now, but I think it is the right time. Our children all joined the church here when they were young.

I am old enough that I can remember the old church building, hearing many great preachers preach, hearing the saints shout "Hallelujah" and 'Amen", and hearing the congregation sing "It's Good Enough For Me".

I have always felt like I belonged here. I hope to continue to serve the LORD from this base as long as I live. Our family has received many blessings from the LORD, and I expect to receive many more.

Attendees - Homecoming at Hopewell
June 22, 1986

Mrs. Leon Allen, Opelika, AL

L. H. Allen, Jr. Gainesville, FL

Lenora Allen, MD, Atlanta, GA

Chris Goggans, Atlanta, GA

Mrs. Lillie Story, Salem, AL

Louis Porch, Salem, AL

Evanelle S. Porch, Salem, AL

John Porch, Salem, AL

Lois M. Moore, Opelika, AL

Lou Moore, Opelika, AL

Rev. Andy Knight, Opelika, AL

Nell Knight, Opelika, AL

Mrs. Irma McConnell, Opelika, AL

Arnold & Doris McConnell, Opelika, AL

Mickey & Ken McConnell, Opelika, AL

Linda, Jerry & Kristi Smallwood, Opelika, AL

Kim S. Ledbetter, Opelika, AL

LaVerne Miller, Opelika, AL

Mr. & Mrs. J. H. Wade, Opelika, AL

Earnest & Jean Whatley, Opelika, AL

Jenny, Curtis & Bryon Whatley, Opelika, AL

Mrs. Mamie Moore, Opelika, AL

Wayne & Juanita Freeman, Opelika, AL

Lynn & Kim Hanson, Opelika, AL

Leslie & Joshua Knight, Opelika, AL

Clyde Foster, Opelika, AL

Ardeth Smith, Opelika, AL

Roy W. Clegg, Opelika, AL

Jewel H. Clegg, Opelika, AL

Jack & Carolyn McConnell, Opelika AL

Jason McConnell, Opelika, AL

Hazel M. Calhoun, Albertville, AL

Jasper & Pat Brown, Opelika, AL

Audrey & Wayne Brown, Opelika, AL

Overene Jones Risher, Rock Hill, SC

Jewel Lynch Buice, Rock Hill, SC

Faye Jones & Miles Lineberger, Rock Hill, SC

Mrs. Carrie C. Moore, Opelika, AL

Earnest & Lillian Paschal, Opelika, AL

Eula Mayberry, Opelika, AL

Travis, Nettie & Steve Letlow, Opelika, AL

Carolyn Colacurto, Pompano Beach, FL

Becky, Jenny & Nancy Colacurto, Pompano Bch

Tom, Kathy & Ben Porch, Pensacola, FL

Ann, Buddy, & Anna Porch, Huntsville, AL

Brad Porch & Billy Rodgers, Huntsville, AL

Nancy Bordeaux, Opelika, AL

Dorothy Bell, Phenix City, AL

Margaret & Rich Dunson, Opelika, AL

Yvonne & Mura Dunson, Opelika, AL

Elizabeth L. & John Vandiver, Cullman, AL

Lora Lynch Orr, Athens, GA

Elise C. & Robert Riddle, Opelika, AL

Lera Foster Chadwick, Opelika, AL

Mrs. Josie Lynch (W. O., Sr.), Shreveport LA

Thelma Lynch Williams, Parkersburg, WV

Becky Oliver, Auburn, AL

Hallie Lee Stoudernmire, Deatsville, AL

Mildred Sims, Maryville, TN

Joe & Nancy Lynch, Shreveport, LA

Millie, Katherine & David Peters, Maryville, TN

Floy W. Waller, Auburn, AL

Kelly Herring, Opelika, AL

Virginia (Mrs. Lynch) Whatley, Opelika, AL

Lurline Smith, Opelika, AL

Diane Blue, Opelika, AL

Ed Smith, Opelika, AL

Charles & Faith Hoople, Columbus, GA

Imogene & Benton Herring, Opelika, AL

Tony Koury, Atlanta, GA

Mrs. Glennie Herring, Opelika, AL

Clayton Roberts, Opelika, AL

Charles Story, Macon, GA

Donald B. Duffey, Jr., Huntsville, AL

Dorothy Story Blackburn, Decatur, GA

Annette Allen Childress, Spartanburg, SC

Edward A. Blackburn, Decatur, GA

Alicia & Maria Childress, Spartanburg, SC

Ken & Carol Story, Opelika, AL

Myrtle J. C. McGhee, Alexander City, AL

John & Jennifer Story, Opelika, AL

Sarah Floyd, Alexander City, AL

Charles & Ann Whatley, Opelika, AL

Perry & Esther Williams & 2 children, Opelika, AL

Tom, Andrew, & Virginia Whatley, Opelika, AL

Susan E. Scott, Opelika, AL

Robin McIntyre, Auburn, AL

Roy & Alice Riddle, Opelika, AL

Lundy & Wilma Fuller, Auburn, AL

Louise Edwards, Auburn, AL

Mrs. Tessie Hinson, Opelika, AL

Mr. & Mrs. Wesley Jackson, LaGrange, GA

Betty & Billy Hightower, Opelika, AL

Jimmy & Faye Tankersley & 2 sons, Opelika, AL

Rev. & Mrs. W. O. Lynch, Jr., New Orleans, LA

Grady & Nellie Mae Chadwick, Opelika, AL

Marie, Arlene & Sherrill Nixon, Auburn, AL

Mable & Jack Gray, Opelika, AL

Rev. & Mrs. Robert Wilson, Montgomery, AL

R. L Yielding, Opelika, AL

Katrena Yielding, Opelika, AL

ORDER OF PRELIMINARIES
10:45 AM

Prelude .... Pianist

Hymn ..... "O For a Thousand Tongues to Sing" ..... #1

Welcome .... Reverend Andy Knight, Pastor
Prayer

Historic Remarks .... Mrs. Estelle Allen
Other Remarks

ORDER OF MORNING WORSHIP

Call to Worship .... Pastor
Invocation .... Reverend Robert Wilson

Hymn ...... "Jesus, with Thy Church Abide" ...... #311
*Affirmation of Faith .... #738

Announcements .... Pastor
Morning Prayer

Offertory
*Doxology .... #809

Introduction of Visitors .... Pastor
    Former Pastors
    Former Members
    Home Church of Relatives
    Jones, Story, Lynch Family Members

Special Music ... "The Old Country Church On The Hill"

Introduction of Morning Speaker
Sermon .... Reverend W.O. Lynch

Hymn .... "And Are We Yet Alive" .... #336

Table Blessing .... Mr. Earnest Paschal
Benediction .... Pastor

ORDER OF AFTERNOON SESSION
1:10 PM

Prelude .... Pianist
Congregational Singing .... Mr. John Porch, Leader

Afternoon Prayer
Extemporaneous Testimonies

Introduction of Afternoon Speaker
Reminiscence .... Reverend Robert Wilson

Hymn .... "Blest Be the Tie That Binds" ...... #306

Expressions of Hope for the Future .... Pastor
Closing Prayer

* * * * * * * * *

WE REMEMBER THOSE WHO HAVE DIED SINCE OUR LAST
HOMECOMING IN 1957

Allen, Leon H.	McConnell, W. Herron
Capps, Ora Riddle	McConnell, Jasper
Chadwick, Julian T.	McConnell, Lionel
Dunn, J.O.	McConnell, Luther
Dorsey, Ruth M.	McConnell, Mary Heath
Foster, Effie	McConnell, Thelma
Foster, Johnnie Mae	Ramsey, Amanda
Foster, Marshall O.	Ramsey, J.G.
Foster, Sam L.	Ramsey, Maude
Herring, Floyd A.	Riddle, Poleman
Herring, Kate	Roberts, Billie McConnell
Herring, Martin L.	Roberts, Eugene C.
Hinson, Clifton S.	Smith, Melvin
Hinson, Luther M.	Story, Ethel
Hinson, Sarah Allen	Story, Jesse F.
Howard, Mary Corley	Story, Mrs. Ocie
Hoople, Ellen Story	Story, Otis
Huff, Mrs. J.T.	Tinsley, Sammie Ramsey
Ledbetter, Jesse L.	Vinson, Agnes
Ledbetter, Mrs. Jesse	Vinson, Ollie Story
McConnell, Adele	Welch, L.C.
McConnell, Curtis	Widener, Willie Hinson
	Wright, N.L.

Memories of Pastors

Estelle Vinson Allen

*"Wherefore seeing we also are compassed about with so great
a cloud of witnesses, let us lay aside every weight, and the sin
which doth so easily beset us, and let us run with patience
the race that is set before us,..."* (Hebrews 12:1KJV)

In 1917, we were living on the Jones farm half-way between Salem and Hopewell Church. Our pastor, **Rev. W. D. Stewart** came to spend the night with us. My sister, Bernice, had a very sore red arm. Brother Stewart diagnosed it as erysipelas. He told Mama to keep it soaked often in Epsom salts water. This she did and the remedy cured the disease. At this time, and for years, the Lee Charge parsonage was at Pine Grove Church. In the 1900's it was the practice for the pastor to come to their once-a- month appointment on a Friday night and spend the night with some member. It was a long drive from Pine Grove to Hopewell by horseback or buggy. This being a Methodist Protestant Church, it was the custom to have the business meeting of the church held on Saturday morning.

****

I remember that **Rev. S. H. "Kim" Lynch** preached the Revival at Hopewell in 1918. That was the summer that Geoffrey Story and I joined the church along with several others, including my brother, Leland Vinson and Geoffrey's brother, W. B. Story.

****

Rev. J. S. Eddins preached our Revival Service in 1921. He was the president of the Alabma Methodist Protestant Conference.

****

Rev. J. C. Casaday preached our service in the summer of 1922. He was president of the Alabma Methodist Protestant Conference that year.

****

In 1923, **Rev. A. C. Messer** was our pastor. I regret that I can't remember him. He only stayed one year.

****

Rev. Arthur Lynch was our pastor in 1924 and 1925. Our new church was built during his term, so there was a lot of activity going on in the church at that time. At a trustee meeting in 1924, five members pledged to donate a grand total of $632.00 toward the new building.

****

Rev. W. C. Conner came in 1926 and served for four years. He was an emotional singer. One song I remember his leading was "He Gave His Life For Me". The chorus went:

> "I gave, I gave, my life for thee,
> What hast thou given to me?
> I've borne, I've borne it all for thee
> What hast thou borned for me?"

This song of long ago has always been emotional to me, as we ask the questions, 'What have we given unto Him?" We must have been singing at a Saturday morning meeting as I do not remember the organ playing while we sang this song.

****

Rev. A. L. Lumpkin came in 1930. He soon re-introduced the Christian Endeavor meetings on Sunday evening. This was very good for the youth and for the church. We had a large number of youth in the church then. He also is credited with helping to organize the Women's Missionary Society in 1931.

****

Sometime later we had a visiting preacher at Hopewell. The Christian Endeavor members were having a contest. The members were divided into two groups and the names were posted on posters. The visiting preacher made a joke about our having Storys, Riddles, Meadows and Hightowers....

****

The main thing I remember about **Rev. E. A. Maddox** is that he married Leon and me January 20, 1935 at 6:00 P. M. at the home of my parents. Our witnesses were Mildred Story and Leland Vinson, and of course, my parents.

****

Rev. Wilbur Walton served as our pastor for five years starting in 1936. He and his wife were loved by all Hopewell members. At the time Rev. Wilbur Walton was our pastor, we did not have a clock on the wall. The church gave him a watch. So that he wouldn't have to stop and hold his arm out to see what time it was, he took his watch off and laid it on the pulpit. Once when he was doing some forceful preaching, he knocked his watch off the pulpit. After the watch hit the floor, there was a minute of silence while he picked up the watch, gained his composure and finished his sermon on time! Maybe this story is why for a long time we have had a clock on the wall for the ministers to see, so they will finish in time.

****

Rev. T. A. Maxey served Lee Circuit in 1942. He and his wife visited us quite often. My son, Hartwell, was fascinated with a handkerchief trick that Brother Maxey did.

****

Rev. Kelly Scott served in 1943 and 1944. Hartwell Allen and Eugene Eastridge joined the church during the summer of 1943. Brother Scott gave baptismal and church memberhip certificates. In 1944, Marion Story, G. L. Story, Jr., Bobby Story, Dorothy Hinson and Annette Allen joined Hopewell Church.

****

Rev. Robert (Bob) Wilson served Lee Charge in 1944-48. He was a wonderful pastor. He and his wife, Carolyn, were loved by all. A large number of people joined the church during that time. One was Richard McConnell. I wonder if Richard remembers that day. Brother Bob came back for a couple of Revivals and gave the afternoon message at the Homecoming in 1986.

The following was taken from an article in the October, 1996, <u>Alabama Christian Advocate</u>.

Wesley Gardens dedicates chapel in memory of Wilson

Consecration services were held September 8th for the Rev. Robert Lee Wilson Memorial Chapel at Wesley Gardens, a United Methodist Home for the Aging located in Montgomery.

Wilson served as the retirement community's first minister. Wilson, who died in 1993, was remembered for his command of the scripture, his sense of humor and his compassion for others.

Bishop Paul Duffey paid tribute to Wilson, remembering him as one who was "given totally to doing the work of God. How fitting it is that this place should be named in memory of this man."

****

Rev. H. F. Wesley served in 1948-49. He was an older minister and was not in school as most of our pastors had been. My brother's family really liked him and his wife; and several of their family joined the church during his pastorate, as did Earnest Paschal and eight others.

****

Rev. Carl Williams came in 1950 and served only one year. His wife was ill in Tuscaloosa, so he lived alone. He visited us and had dinner with us several times. He was transferred to North Alabama Conference.

****

Rev. Glenn Sirmon came to Lee Circuit in 1951-1953. Annette was playing the piano at Hopewell at this time. He was invited to come back and preach at our Homecoming in 1957.

****

Rev. James Love served in 1954. This is the year Hopewell started paying for a subscription to the Alabama Christian Advocate for resident members at $1.13 per year. By 1995, the cost had risen to $10 per year. This project was canceled in 1997 after 42 years.

****

In 1955, Lee Circuit was changed. Pine Grove and Beulah became a charge with Rev. Love as the pastor. Lee Charge now consisted of Hopewell, Morris Chapel and Pierce Chapel. **Rev. Charles Pittman** was assigned to be our Pastor. We had no parsonage and I remember that Rev. Pittman stayed some of the time with Mrs. D. P. Meadows while the parsonage was being built. He also lived part time in a house owned by Ernest Chappell. Some of the leaders who worked to get a parsonage built were Mr. Herbert Walton, Mr. Travis Letlow, Mr. Ernest Chappell and Mr. Leon Allen.

****

Rev. Gillis Crenshaw served in 1958 and 1959 as pastor. He and his wife were our very good friends. He seemed to like our people and the beauty of Hopewell. At our revival in July, 1996, our visiting minister, Rev. George Mathison, mentioned remembering and knowing Rev. Crenshaw. He probably came to the area meetings of Methodist Youth Fellowship at Hopewell during that time.

****

Somewhere around this time, the ministers were assigned to their pastorates in June instead of January.

****

In 1963, **Rev. Robert Hall** served three months; then **Rev. Sam Lowery** was appointed to the Charge. As far as I remember, he was the only pastor to invite a missionary to come speak to us. Rev. Lowery and probably Uncle Jesse Story built a portable frame to erect a world mission map for the speaker to use. It was November 19, 1963, when Dr. Thocoma, President of Luchnow Christian College in India, came to Hopewell to tell us about the mission work there. Another special thing I remember hearing Rev. Lowery say was that when he went to see Mrs. Ethel Deas Story (local shut-in) to minister to her, he always came away feeling that he had been ministered to by Mrs. Story's example and prayer.

****

Rev. Linwood Lewis was appointed to Lee Charge in 1963. He stayed one year and might have finished Emory that year. He spent some time at the Conference Headquarters in Andalusia and is now retired.

****

Rev. Dick Cobb served in 1965-66. I remember he performed the wedding ceremony of Marietta Story and Robin McIntyre in June 1966.

****

Rev. David Chunn came to us in 1967 and was appointed to Wesley Memorial in Opelika in 1968. He performed Lenora's and Jimmy Goggan's wedding ceremony at Wesley United Methodist church in 1969. Faith Hoople and Lauren Duffey were flower girls.

****

Rev. Bobby Holiday served Lee Circuit from 1968-70. He encouraged our leaders to attend training meetings. Leon attended several and was very encouraged. Rev. Holiday demonstrated how to take the church offerings and had ushers help when the congregation partook of holy communion. At this time, our pastor came to Hopewell two Sunday mornings and two Sunday evenings for worship. This gave the pastor and his family time to take part in our activities. I remember that he visited different Sunday School classes. He and his wife had two boys in my junior Sunday School class.

****

Rev. C. D. Monday was appointed to us in 1971. Rev. Monday had received a call to preach late in life. He and his wife gave up their jobs and started out. He had a lovely wife who could give inspirational talks. They helped start a choir again as their daughter could play the piano. Rev. Monday was a Northerner. He had met his wife at Maxwell Airfield in Montgomery, where he was stationed and where she worked. He told the story about the first time that he went to see Mary Ellen's family. For bread at supper that night, they had a hoecake of cornbread. This was unfamiliar to him. Since he was a guest, the uncut hoecake was passed to him first. He did not know the "Southern" custom was to break himself a piece of bread and pass it on! (*In the retelling of story, Mama does not tell what he did, other than to say he was embarrassed.*) aae.

****

Rev. Robert Warren was our pastor from 1973-1974. He was here in 1974 when Mrs. Dorsey disappeared. On that Sunday afternoon, he and a large group of members met at our home for prayer.

****

Rev. Phil Craddock served 1975-1976. It was during this time that our fifth Sunday joint services were started and the offering was to go for maintenance of our parsonage.

****

Rev. Judd Stinson was called to preach after several years in a successful business field. He only served on Lee Circuit for one year. He ate lunch with us often. He finished Emory and went as associate minister to Auburn First Methodist.

****

Philip McVay, our lovable young minister, served four years from 1979-1983. Betty and Billy Hightower treated him like a son. Betty would often go and clean the parsonage for him. I went with her a few times. He ate lunch with us quite often. Sometimes he would bring his brother who was in school in Auburn. We loved Philip very much.

****

Rev. Eugene Hall served in 1983-1984. I went with him several times to visit some of the shut-in members. They also ate lunch with us often. His oldest daughter, Tanya, sends me a Christmas card each year. She married February 21, 1998, to Dr. Seth Connor. They live in Pompano Beach, FL.

****

Rev. Andy Knight came in 1985 and served through 1989. I thought he was a very dedicated Christian. Ellen Story Hoople died soon after he came. He conducted her funeral with compassion. Leon died in October,

1985, and he was most sympathetic with our family. He came often to see me to talk of our church interest. Wherever he is, I wish him the LORD's blessing.

****

In 1989 came **Rev. Andy Gartman** and his cheerful and helpful wife, Patricia. They had some stressful times as many families in today's world do. Andy was in school at Emory and became very interested in singing there. It was helpful to Hopewell to have a good song leader. So far as I know he was our only pastor who went with a group to another area to help build a new church. Patricia was a great UMW member. She served as vice president while here.

****

Rev. Gene May came in June, 1993. He had many goals for Hopewell, but did not stay long enough to help carry them out.

****

In January, 1995, **Rev. Daniel Randall**, came. He was full of vision and hope for Hopewell Chruch. One emphasis in 1996 was the celebration of the church's 150th Anniversary, June 23rd. Rev. Randall married Miss Tay Granger in June, 1996.

****

Comments:

Since 1995, the three churches on Lee Circuit have been Hopewell, Morris Chapel and Pierce Chapel. While Rev. Philip Craddock was pastor in 1975, a joint worship service was started for each Fifth Sunday. It had several purposes. One was for fellowship. However, there was a need for an ongoing maintenance fund for the Lee Circuit parsonage. It was mutually decided to start meeting together and the offering that Sunday would go for parsonage needs. Also, the pastor could be with all of his "flock" each fifth Sunday. After about 20 years, some wanted to change this plan. Harmony was reached and each church has its own fifth Sunday service with the offering still going for parsonage maintenance. Along with this change was a suggestion that each church plan for one chargewide service during the year. Hopewell sponsors the Easter Sunrise Service for its worship and fellowship chargewide service. (Alicia Spado)

*Annette's note : Obviously there have been more pastors at Hopewell since 1995. Although Mama did not include more in her original notes, I will include them in the list of pastors at the end of this book.

Memories of Some Men

(Honorable Mention of a few Non-members)
(No special order, more or less in the order she thought of them…)
Estelle Vinson Allen

I don't remember too much about the older men at Hopewell. I do know they sat in an area called the "amen corner". Some were Ben McConnell, Billy Jones, W. S. Lisle, Tom Browning, Jim Littleton and my Grandpa Story (Judge Aaron).

****

One old man that I remember slightly was a **Mr. Crawford**. He came walking into the church leaning on his cane, dressed in an old frock tail coat. He was a retired school teacher. As a child, I did not notice this, but I remember hearing some of the older women say that his white shirt cuffs were very, very frazzled. Mr. Crawford stood when he prayed. He seemed to be very feeble and he probably was too weak to kneel. I believe his wife always sat with him. *(After looking at old 1903 records, I think this was Mr. James Crawford and that his wife was Mrs. Fanny Crawford.)* aae

****

I am sure **Mr. B. A. U. (Ben) McConnell** (1839-1921) sat in the "amen corner", but I do not remember how he looked as I do the others. I am sure he was there because his name appears often in the minutes from 1912-1916. Maybe he was the one with a beard. Mr. McConnell served in the

Civil War (CSA – 1862 – Co. K, 34th Alabama Infantry). Having been born in 1839, he was probably the oldest man I ever saw.

****

I saw **Mr. Jim Littleton** (1858-1946) a number of times. He was a faithful member at Hopewell. Once I heard Otis Story say a long time ago that Mr. Littleton said "If the Bible said a whale swallowed Jonah, then it was so."

****

I don't remember much about **Uncle Tom Browning** (1859-1926). He married Grandpa Story's sister, Aunt Fannie. From old church records, he seemed to be present at the business meetings of the church and his name appears on several lists of officers. I remember going to a small pond behind their house. It looked big to me for I had never seen that much water. Also, they had several sycamore trees in their front yard. I never saw another yard quite like that. Once when we were going by their house late one warm evening, he was sitting on the kitchen steps, eating. Someone said he was eating cornbread and milk for supper. (Sometimes I eat cornbread and milk for supper.)

****

I remember how **Uncle Billy Jones** (William Carter Jones, 1845-1919) looked, but nothing else. His name also appears several times in our old minutes records between 1912 and 1916. He married Grandpa Story's sister, Artimissi Antionette Story, whom we called Aunt Nette. His obituary, written by Mrs. Frances Jane Story (Fannie) Browning, sister of his wife, for <u>The Alabama Christian Advocate</u> in 1919, included this paragraph:

A paragraph from his Obituary:

"In Brother Jones, we have a model type of those characters, against whom 'the gates of hell shall not prevail'. Only once before has the writer known an individual of whom it was said, 'He has not an enemy in the world'. And, O such patience; such Christian fortitude! His church was his pride, to say the least. In the removal of this dear brother, the world at large has lost a jewel that it, perhaps, failed to appreciate."

****

Mr. John F. Lynch (1867-1940), chairman of committee to collect money to build a new church, reported on October 18, 1924, that $632.00 had been collected. (taken from minutes)

****

I don't think **Mr. John Leland Allen** (April 1868 – May 1937) was ever late to a church meeting. In old records, his name is on 1913 membership roll and he is listed as a steward in 1914. Mr. Allen supported Hopewell Church and probably attended more quarterly conferences at other churches than any other member. One remark I heard him say once was that he liked "comers", but he also liked "goers". They had a big black walnut tree in their yard. One picture I remember of him is sitting under the tree on a warm day with his sun hat on. Mr. Allen lost his life in a car accident in 1937.

****

Mr. Jim Tom McConnell (1868-1939) led the singing at Hopewell for quite a number of years. He loved to sing and was a good singer and leader.

Singing class taught by Jim Tom McConnell

****

W. S. Lisle (1870-_?___) came to us from Georgia. I am sure he was among those in the "amen corner", but I do not remember much about him.

****

Alto Story (1896-1936) was in World War I and settled in Birmingham, Alabama, after the war, so I never knew him very well. However, later I knew his family quite well. His son Charles Story visited my family when he was a teenager and he learned to love Hopewell. Alto was stationed in England with Company I, 4th Regiment Casuals as an engine fitter with the air service during World War I. His serial number was 1067-734. He received an honorable discharge on December 21, 1918.

Alto Story in service uniform (back row, right)

****

Uriah Lee Story (1877-1941) is listed on the oldest membership record we have, 1903. He probably joined long before then. In our old records, he is shown as a class leader in 1913 and a trustee in 1916. I can remember when he held many different jobs in the church. His children were active in Hopewell Church as long as they lived nearby. He had an accidental death.

****

My father, **Marcellus Neal Vinson** (May 1, 1882 – February 2, 1949) joined Hopewell Church in 1904. Old records show that he was a steward in 1912 and a trustee in 1917. My father was a lover of nature. I remember he would often take walks in the woods on Sunday mornings. My husband told me once that he had been with Mr. Vinson and a group of men and that Mr. Vinson was the cleanest spoken man in the group. I considered that a great tribute. I know Papa loved his family.

I use Proverbs 22:1 (KJV) to describe Papa.
"A good name is to be chosen rather than great riches."

****

I remember **Mr. Herron McConnell** (1895-1975) coming to church and sitting in a similar place as where **Arnold McConnell** (1926-2005) sits now (1996). I remember the Sunday they came together and Arnold joined the church.

****

I remember **Mr. Sam Foster** (1878-1972) always helped with the graves for many families after the funerals. I am sure a lot of the concrete graves are some of his work. I remember he was a great entertainer with his tales.

****

Mr. Daniel Porter Meadows (1889-1951) was not a member of our church, but was a supporter. He came often and was a great help when the new church was built in 1925.

****

Jesse F. Story (1893-1971) joined Hopewell at an early age and was a leader all his life. He was the secretary for the quarterly conference for a long time. In the early days, our appointment time for the pastor was on the Third Saturday and Sunday of each month. A quarterly conference was held at Hopewell on the third Saturday in May each year. In the morning, there was preaching. At noon, a big dinner was spread on tables under trees across the road from the church. In the afternoon, conference was held, with all the churches giving reports of their condition. Uncle Jesse was active in Hopewell Church in many ways. He was an active steward, which at one time had the job of collecting the pastor's salary. He was superintendent of the Sunday School for many years and also taught a class. He was a skilled carpenter and built the pulpit and communion table. His mantra might have been: "Pray for a good harvest, but keep on plowing."

****

One of the saddest things that I remember ever happening in our area was Sunday night, March 27, 1955, when **Emmett Poulas** (1936-1955) was killed in an auto accident. He died April 1st. Three young men were on their way to MYF at Hopewell when they collided with a car being driven by a drunk driver on the wrong side of the road. The other two were **Clayton Roberts** (1935-) and **Jack McConnell** (1937-). They were seriously injured, but survived and have had permanent related conditions. They have also continued to be active members at Hopewell.

****

Jasper McConnell (1902-1983) was a fine man in our community and church. He and his wife, Emma, deeded an acre of land to the Hopewell Cemetery.

****

Otis Story (1897-1984) joined the church as a young boy and supported it all his life. He held many offices in the church, such as chairman of the board, trustee for the cemetery, lay leader and he helped teach the Browning Sunday School Class. He probably helped with the cemetery improvement more than anyone besides Ellen Story Hoople.

From a Hebrew prayer:
"Hear O Israel, the LORD is our God, the LORD is One.
Blessed be His name, whose glorious kingdom is forever and ever."

****

It seems that I remember **Luther Hinson** (1897-1970) and **Clifton Hinson** (1903-1973) together. They seemed the most congenial brothers that I ever knew. They were known as good neighbors.

"He was a friend of man, and lived in a house
by the side of the road." *Homer*

****

Charles V. Story (1925-1992), son of Alto and Will Morrison Story, was not a member at Hopewell, but he loved it from a young age and supported it in his early adulthood. Some of the money he sent to Hopewell Church was used to buy our pulpit chairs.

****

Leon Hartwell Allen, Sr. was born March 27, 1911, and joined Hopewell Church in 1918. He married Estelle Vinson on January 20, 1935, and died October 24, 1985. I think his favorite Bible verse was: "Thy word is a lamp unto my feet and a light unto my path." (Psalms 119:105KJV). He was a lamplighter at home and at church. All his adult life, he built the fire in winter and lit the lamps in the evenings at Hopewell. After we got central heat and air in the church, he would go early on Sunday morning when necessary to get the church comfortable in time for services. He held several different offices at Hopewell and was delegate to Annual Conference several times. He was a willing contributor to the finances of the church. He lived his vows to God, to family and his church. I have heard Leon refer to this verse: "He that tilleth his land shall have plenty of bread."(Proverbs 28:19a*KJV*)

To Leon:
"The world is full of folks, it's true,
But there was only one of you."
From "Miss You", Author Unknown

****

Walter Clegg (1921-1987) was a good friend of ours. He joined Hopewell Church in 1948 and loved it the rest of his life. He was Chairman of the Board of Trustees from 1980-1986. He was also in charge of the upkeep of the cemetery. Walter was largely responsible financially and physically for installing the stained glass diamond-shaped window in the front gable of the church. It is quite impressive at night with the spotlight on it. I'm not sure he was ever properly recognized for this contribution. Walter served in the U. S. Navy from 1942-1945 during World War II. He was stationed in the Pacific Ocean on the battleship USS Mississippi as a Boatsman-Mate Second Class.

"From rocks and sand and every ill,
May God preserve the sailor still."
Daniel Schwartz

****

Poleman V. Riddle (1902-1972), son of Willa Nettie Story and Emmett Eugene Riddle, was a veteran of World War II, serving from 1942-1945 in French North Africa as a mechanic repairman of turret engines for the Air Corps. He was a member of Hopewell until his death and he is buried in Hopewell Cemetery.

****

Louie Porch (1922-1992) joined Hopewell in 1949. He and his wife, Evanelle Story, were supporters of Hopewell for all the years they lived in other areas of the country. After he retired and moved near Hopewell, he was active in all areas of the church. To me, Louie seemed like a very happy and contented person. I am sure one of his greatest interests was his family. Sometime after Evanelle died, when several of us were talking, he said something like this: "I feel like Evanelle was one person that was prepared to leave this life when that time came."

****

Mr. P. L. Pope (1886-1977) was not a member at Hopewell, but he attended often. I remember him more as a person than his coming to church. The first time I saw him was about 1936. He and Leon were working on a county cotton program and he ate lunch with us. I was captivated by his dry humor. From that time on, I claimed him as a friend.

****

Mr. and Mrs. J. T. Huff (Mr. Huff 1903-1996) transferred their membership from Trinity in Opelika to Hopewell on March 25, 1956. Mr. Huff was treasurer of the parsonage fund for several years. They were supporters of the Browning Sunday School Class. They gave a nice desk for the class. Mrs. Huff died in 1984. Their daughter, Eula Will Huff Mayberry, has been a dear friend and supportive member of Hopewell since 1956.

****

Ed Koziski (1933-1996) was a member at Hopewell only a few years, but he endeared himself to its members as did his caring wife, Edith. Ed died in March, 1996, after a long illness.

"He grew toward the light."
Source Unknown

****

My dear nephew, **Wayne Freeman**, born October 31, 1929, died this morning, May 29, 1996. I mourn his death. I wish he could have lived longer to have been with family, relatives and friends. His memory and smile will live with us always. Wayne was my very good friend. Wayne joined Hopewell in 1945 while Rev. Wilbur Walton was our pastor. He had become a rock at Hopewell and will be greatly missed. He was a lover of the country as were his ancestors, so he lay down in the arms of Mother Nature. The tears flow down my cheeks unbidden. Friday, May 31, 1996. I went to Wayne's funeral service at Hopewell this afternoon. It was a lovely service of songs, prayer and praise. The flowers were beautiful and the church was overflowing with family and friends.

I want to inscribe this verse of Scripture to him:
"Precious in the sight of the LORD is the death of his saints."
Psalms 116:15(KJV)

I am writing this mainly to tell about Wayne Freeman showing concern and interest in family and my safety. About two months before Wayne died, I had found pictures of most all of Mama's children and grandchildren as of 1954. I did not remember that I had them. One day when Wayne came by (which he did frequently), I showed them to him and mentioned that I was going to get some copies made. Wayne said he wanted some. When I got them, I called to tell him they were here. On May 21, 1996, he came by to get them, but I did not answer the doorbell. That morning, I had been cutting some briars and bushes and found some "hidden" roses. I always called them "Mama's roses". I don't know where she got the bush, but it was large and had a purplish color bloom, unlike any others that I have seen. Mrs. Poe, my neighbor, is always giving me things so I decided to take her one of Mama's roses. She and Mama were good friends. When I got back from Mrs. Poe's, I decided to tie up another rose bush. Leon never threw anything away, so I knew I could find some old hay strings down at the hay shed. I spent some time there looking for twine, a sharp pointed tool to drive a hole, a stave to drive in the ground, and a tool to "hit" it with. Then, as I was coming back around the northwest side of my house, Mr. and Mrs. Poe were driving into my yard. As I was going to meet them, I saw Wayne's truck in my yard. Wayne had rung the doorbell, knocked and got no answer. He saw my car and wondered where I was so went to check at my neighbor's. Since I had just been over there, they, too, wondered about me and came over to check on me. What concern! Wayne got his pictures and I will always remember this last special visit.

Thank you, Wayne, from your Aunt Estelle.

****

In honor of my brother, **Leland Morgan Vinson** (1906-1998), namesake of Lester Leland Vinson and Laborn Morgan Story, I am including this song. Many years ago, I heard him say that it was one of his favorite songs.

I Feel Like Traveling On
Yes, I feel like traveling on, I feel like traveling on;
My heavenly home is bright and fair, I feel like traveling on.
………...
"Happy is the man whose wish and care
And few paternal acres bound
Content to breathe his native air
There in his own ground."
From "Ode to Solitude" by Alexander Pope

****

Another supporter of Hopewell Church was **Andrew C. Story** (1918-2003), even though he was not a member. Andrew, we are truly grateful for your generous support over the years.

****

Earnest C. Paschal, Sr. (1922-2016) is the only living member of Hopewell Church that fought in World War II. I admire and revere him and all veterans. Earnest served in the Army from 1943 until his honorable discharge in 1945. After completing basic and other training at Camp Lee,

VA, in April 1944, Earnest left for the Pacific Theater. By August, 1944, he was with the 1st Calvary Division, 7th Reg, Troup E and was invading the Philippines and helping to free POW's held there in September, 1944. He served as a light mortar gunner and a radio carrier. They slept wherever and whenever they could, ditches, old buildings, trucks, foxholes… In March, 1945, he was wounded south of Manila, hospitalized, and discharged in May, 1945. He was awarded numerous medals including The Purple Heart. Earnest has been a staunch supporter and attendee at Hopewell since his stint in the Army. He is loved and revered by all who know him.

****

Charles Hoople (1914-1997) was in the military during World War II, but he was not overseas during conflict. He served some time at the prison of war camp in Opelika guarding German prisoners. While he was stationed in Opelika, he met and married Barbara Ellen Story. Charles was from Canada and his family moved to California when he was still a boy.

****

I want to mention a special friend of Leon's, **Paul Hinson** (1913-1936). Paul met an untimely death due to an auto accident in 1935. He is buried at Watoola United Methodist Church. He was the younger brother of Luther and Clifton and son of Loyd E. Hinson (1890-1953).

****

Geoffrey Lee Story, Sr. (1911-2002) was selected Father of the Year in 1996. Geoffrey joined Hopewell in July, 1918, attended and supported Hopewell until his death. He and his wife, Mary Allen Story, reared a large family of five boys and one girl. Mary died in 1988. Soon after, Geoffrey married the former Helen Thompson. She was a member at Pine Grove United Methodist Church and they shared their Sundays between the two churches.

****

James Donald Mullins (1927-2007) is a faithful member and caretaker of the grounds. His sons, Tim, Lee and Don have been good stewards for the LORD as well.

****

I must mention two more nephews who have been faithful to Hopewell. **Kelly K. Freeman** (1931-___) and his wife **Margaret Hamilton Freeman** (1932-___) have not lived in this area, but have been financially supportive and have retained their membership here. **William "Billy" Freeman** (1943-___), my sister's youngest child, is still quite active in the church.

****

Men mentioned in Memories of MEN of Hopewell

Alphabetical listing

Allen, John Leland (1868-1937

Allen, Leon Hartwell, Sr. (1911-1985)

Browning, Thomas H. (Tom) (1859-1926)

Clegg, Roy Walter (1921-1987)

Crawford, _____ (1851-__?__ (possibly James R., d. 1920)

Foster, Samuel L. (Sam) (1878-1972)

Freeman, Kelly Keith (1931-_____) and wife, Margaret Howard Freeman (1932-_____)*

Freeman, Wayne (1929-1996)

Freeman, William (Billy) (1943-_____)

Herring, Floyd A. (1888-1965)

Hinson, Clifton S. (1903-1973)

Hinson, Luther M. (1897-1970)

Hinson, Paul Cyrus (1913-1936)

---

* Mrs. J. T Huff and Margaret Freeman listed here because they are mentioned with their husbands.

Hoople, Charles (1914-1997)

Huff, J. T. (1903-1996) and Mrs. Huff (1905-1984)*

Jones, William Carter (Billy) (1845-1919)

Koziski, Ed (1933-1996)

Lisle, William S. (1870-___)

Littleton, James W. (Jim) (1858-1953)

Lynch, John F. (1867-1940)

McConnell, William <u>Arnold</u> (1926-2005)

McConnell, Benjamin A. U. (Ben) (1839-1921)

McConnell, William <u>Herron</u> (1895-1975)

McConnell, Jack (1937-____)

McConnell, Jasper D. (1902-1983)

McConnell, James T. (Jim Tom) (1868-1939)

Meadows, Daniel Porter III (D.P.) (1889-1951)

Mullins, James Donald (1927-2007)

Paschal, Earnest Clifton, Sr. (1922-2016)

Pope, P. L. (1886-1977)

Porch, Louie E. (1922-1992)

Poulas, Emmett (1936-1955)

Riddle, Poleman V. (1902-1972)

Roberts, Clayton (1935-____)

Story, Alto (1896-1936)

Story, Andrew C. (1918-2003)

Story, Charles V. (1925-1992)

Story, Geoffrey Lee, Sr. (1911-2002)

Story, Jesse F. (1893-1971)

Story, Judge Aaron (1849-1922)

Story, Otis Cadenhead (1897-1984)

Story, Uriah Lee (1877-1941)

Vinson, M. N. (Dock) (1882-1949)

Women I Remember

By Estelle V. Allen

It seems the first one I remember most was **Mrs. Frances Story Browning** (1853-1922), my Aunt Fannie. She probably was the first woman leader at Hopewell. In earlier times, women did not hold an office in the church. Old minute records show that she was Sunday School Superintendent and teacher. She was also a writer. She wrote news items to the Methodist Advocate (we called it the "church paper") including obituaries. The reason my mother had so many family obituaries was because different ones had cut them from the "church paper". My mother and I continued to send notices of deaths to the Advocate until that column was discontinued, to my chagrin. I paid for the ones I sent to be published. What I really remember about my Great Aunt Fannie was her testifying, singing and shouting in church. I remember going to their home and seeing a harp in the corner of the room. I had never seen one before. In her obituary, her daughter, Mrs. Gemmie Browning Meadows, mentioned her great prayer life and devotion to Hopewell Church and community. Near the end of her life, her one request was for a white robe.

Rev. 22:17 KJV
"And the Spirit and the bride say, Come.
And let him that heareth say, Come.
And let him that is athirst, Come.
And whosoever will,
Let him take the water of life freely."

****

One of Aunt Fannie's sisters, **Artimissi Antionette (Nettie) Story Jones** (1845-1927) was also a singer and shouter at Hopewell Church. I remember how she looked, but I don't remember much else about her. Leon often told the story about when he was small and went to their house. He was eating dinner there and they had chicken and dumplings. She and Uncle Billy Jones had two sons, Seaborn and Andrew, who became Methodist ministers, and one of their daughters, Nora Louise (Lulu) married Rev. S.H. (Kim) Lynch, also a Methodist minister. Their other daughter, Emma, married John Leland Allen. (Note from Annette: Her name is spelled Antinettie on her grave, but Mama has always believed her name was really Antionette. I was named Annette after her.)

****

Another of Aunt Fannie's sisters, **Miss Leonora (Nora) Story** (1850-1934), was always present at church, but I don't think she shouted. I thought she looked aristocratic. Aunt Nora was a school teacher. We have a copy of one of her contracts. Later, she had a small store in one room of her mother's house from which she sold over the counter medicines and was helpful to those that were sick. She cared for her mother during Great, Great Grandma Ellen's last years. Aunt Nora lived longer than her sisters, so I remember her better. In her later years, she lived with her niece, Mrs. Gemmie Browning Meadows. She influenced my decision to become a teacher and I respected her so much that we named our youngest daughter, Lenora, as her namesake.

****

In about 1920, I remember **Mrs. Esther Lynch Whatley** (1973-1950) going by our house with a daughter, Fannie Mae, on their way to Hopewell for Saturday services. In my mother's memories, she mentioned that Miss Esther Lynch was a Sunday School teacher at Hopewell in the 1890's. She was a life-long member of Hopewell, as were many of that Lynch family. I always thought she was such a pleasant and happy person. Her name is on the 1903 membership roll.

****

There are not many of us left who remember **Miss Betty Word** (1869-1951). She was a tall lady who walked a mile or more to church. She was known as the Sunday School "card class" teacher by many. (Annette's note: I remember going with Grandma Vinson to visit Miss Betty Word at home after she could no longer come to church. I do not remember who took us, but it was before I learned to drive. I was shocked to see there were holes in her floors, there were no screens, the chickens were free to roam in the house, and so to learn that there were many people less fortunate than we were.)

Psalm 118:24 NRSV
"This is the day the LORD has made;
Let us rejoice and be glad in it."

****

Now I remember **Grandma Sultana Story** (1857-1953) quite well. She married my grandfather, Judge Aaron Story, in 1892, taking on the responsibility of being a mother to five of his six motherless children. I never heard Grandma sing or shout at church, but I think she was a good wife, mother and neighbor. I don't remember that she went to Sunday School, but she cooked many, many, many dinners for the pastors, relatives and friends. Buddy and I remember there wasn't much chicken left when it finally came time for the children to eat—mostly the feet! I remember staying some at Grandma Story's house as a child, maybe from one Sunday to the next. Grandma would often walk to visit different people. Once I went with her to see Mr. Rob Freeman, who was sick. Someone was fanning the flies away with a peach tree limb. I remember walking out to the cemetery with her and some other old women. Seemed a long way to a little girl, but it really wasn't very far. Grandma could go visiting, come home, and cook a fast, good, hot dinner before time to ring the dinner bell. She could shuck the longest ears of field corn the fastest I ever saw, cut it, put it in a frying pan and cook it on top of the stove, then put more wood in the stove to get it hot to cook cornbread. She put milk and eggs in her cornbread, beat it smooth and poured it into a greased hot enameled frying pan and put it in the oven. Sometimes she would cook small squash on top of the green beans. Grandma had a small garden fenced in with palings. I'm sure it was full of vegetables, but all I remember were the herbs on one side of the gate and flowers on the other side. Two herbs she always had were horehound and sage. When Grandma's sister came to see her, they talked and laughed and seemed to have a good time. *(Annette's notes: Guess this is where my Grandma Ollie Vinson got her love of visiting the shut-ins of the community. Also, we called Grandma Story's sister Cousin Hester. She was married to my grandmother Allen's brother, so she was really my great aunt, by marriage.)*

For Grandma Story:
"Some do not speak their witness, but they live their witness."

****

Emma Jones Allen (1869-1925) married John Leland Allen in 1907. I heard my mother say that when her mother died in 1891, (Mama was not quite 7), that Emma came to their house to help out some. I have heard different people say that she was a very good seamstress. They had three children, Sara, Leon and Mary Allen. They were life-long dedicated members of Hopewell Church.

****

Records show that **Miss Sammie Ramsey** (1890-1969) was our first organist. The church bought an organ in 1907. She played with much flair. Sometime in the 1920's, her family bought a car, which was unusual in our community. She drove that car up to the church with the same confidence. *(Apparently she was always called Miss Sammie Ramsey, although she did later marry a **Tinsley**.)*

****

Miss Alma Foster (1902-1944) was the organist at Hopewell after Miss Sammie Ramsey. She was a dedicated member of Hopewell and the Women's Missionary Society. She walked a long way to come to meetings.

****

Louise Ramsey Roberts (1909-1988) was a dear friend and loyal member of Hopewell and the Women's Missionary Society (now UMW). I have heard my mother say that she and Louise saw "the Light alike". She served with Mama on the Spiritual Life Committee and they did a lot of visiting together in the community. From her obituary: "Louise was a devoted wife, a sacrificing mother, a happy dedicated Christian and a caring friend. She will be missed by all."

Matthew 5:5 KJV
"Blessed are the meek, for they shall inherit the earth."

****

Another good member of Hopewell Church was **Miss Mildred Story** (1908-1976). The first job I know she had at Hopewell was to help collect money to build the new building in 1924-25. In 1930, she helped collect money to buy a piano and she became our pianist. She was a leader in Christian Endeavor and expected the best from you. I expect the young people learned more Bible verses and location of Books in the Bible than any group since at Hopewell. Sometime about 1940, she gave the church $50 to buy some Cokesbury Worship Hymnals. When Mildred moved to Columbus to teach, she was truly missed at Hopewell. She was secretary for the Jones-Lynch-Story Reunion until she died in 1976. She was my friend from childhood.

****

From membership records, **Willie V. Littleton** (1895-1956) joined the church in 1914. She was the daughter of Mr. and Mrs. Jim Littleton. I don't remember seeing her but a few times, but when I do remember her, she was always very neatly dressed. She married **Mr. Anson Rudd** in 1920. When she died, he gave $1,000 to the Hopewell Cemetery Fund to be invested for upkeep of the cemetery. This is recorded in the minutes of December 14, 1966. (In the minutes of January, 1968, a gift of $1000 is recorded as an anonymous donation to the Cemetery Fund, which I believe came from Mr. Rudd also.)

****

Mrs. Ruth Murphree Dorsey (1906-1974) was a great help to Hopewell. She joined our church at a time when we did not have a pianist and she was a good musician. She also taught the Young Adult Sunday School Class. But her life was blotted out on August 17, 1974. It was the week of Revival. Mrs. Dorsey lived alone and we went by her house each night to take her to church. The last song we sang that Friday night was "God Will Take Care of You." On Saturday morning she came by our house on the way to the store and brought us a delicious banana pudding. Then on Sunday when she was not at Sunday School, someone went to check on her and we learned the sad account of her mysterious disappearance. She has been greatly missed by her friends and relatives.

****

Miss Frances Meadows (1921-1981) was a very active in Christian Endeavor at Hopewell and was the pianist for several years. I remember her being full of humor, as were her parents, Mr. and Mrs. D P. Meadows.

****

My mother, **Laura Olivia Story Vinson** (1884-1980), was a well-known leader at Hopewell Church. She joined the church at an early age and was a member for 84 years. She was Sunday School Superintendent for 20 years and taught the kindergarten class for 45 years. She was active in the Missionary Society, now the United Methodist Women, for 49 years. She served several times as President, but her greatest service to the community was serving as our Spiritual Life Secretary. She was a loyal church member, attending, praying, serving, and giving her best to her LORD and Savior.

"When a Christian's cup is full,
He can do nothing but drink deeply from it,
And praise the LORD for his goodness."

****

Another great leader at Hopewell was **Mrs. Gemmie Browning Meadows** (1887-1956). I remember her praying very earnest prayers. She always knelt as she prayed. This was an old custom and she was the last woman I remember using this humble position. She was the church secretary for a long time and kept up the membership roll. She brought her children to church and they were active in the Christian Endeavor. She was a long time teacher of the Browning Sunday School Class. She died suddenly while teaching this class on Sunday, December 30, 1956.

Mark 13:33 KJV
"Take ye heed, watch and pray:
For ye know not when the time is."

****

My Sister-in-Law, **Agnes Howard Vinson** (1918-1983), was raised in North Carolina. She married my brother, Leland Morgan Vinson, in Ashville, NC, January 25, 1936. They moved to this area in the early 1940's. She later joined the church at Hopewell. She seemed to accept us "down here". She and Mama seemed to get along well and she would often carry Mama visiting in the community. Agnes taught the Primary Class for a number of years and later a Youth Sunday School Class. She was a devoted wife and a loving mother.

****

Sara Allen Hinson (1909-1985) was one of the most dependable persons I have ever known. She worked for her family and for her church. This is one story of her life that will show how dedicated we were to the Women's Missionary Society. In March, 1937, she drove their car to a missionary meeting in Montgomery. Get this picture: There we sit in Capital Heights

Methodist Protestant Church. Her little girl, Dorothy, is sitting in her lap and my little boy, Hartwell, is sitting in my lap! But we are at the meeting! I don't remember that we had any problems with our children. How many mothers could or would do that today???

For Sara, I give you an Irish Proverb:
"It is easy to give half the potato when there is love."

****

Mrs. Willie Hinson Widener (1903-1985) was another long-time member and supporter of Hopewell. I remember her as a very pleasant and giving person. She died soon after Sara died.

****

Evanelle Story Porch (1925-1987) wasn't allowed to live her three score and ten. She and her family were supporters of Hopewell Church for years even though they lived in other areas: Mexico, Missouri, Mississippi, then back to Alabama, Mobile and Montgomery. After her husband, Louie, retired, they built a nice home near her parents, Otis and Lillie Story. Then they became very involved in serving at Hopewell. She served as Sunday School Superintendent and Sunday School class teacher, as well as President of the United Methodist Women's group. She and Louie had four children: Buddy, Carolyn, Tommy, and John. Evanelle was my relative and my friend.

Matthew 5:9 KJV
"Blessed are the peacemakers:
For they shall be called the children of God."

****

Mary Allen Story (1914-1987), my sister-in-law, a happy smiling person, held a number of offices at Hopewell, was a leader in the MYF and served several times as President of the Women's Society of Christian Service and the United Methodist Women. She and Geoffrey had a large family and all were involved in Hopewell Church when they were young.

To Mary
"Be Happy, It is a Way of Life" (Collette)

****

Lillie Thomas Story (1902-1989) and Otis Story were married in 1923. They had one daughter, Evanelle. Aunt Lillie was a communion steward for many years. She was a devoted member of the Browning Sunday School Class and served as treasurer for a number of years. It was a very rare Sunday if Aunt Lillie and Uncle Otis were not in the pew at Hopewell Church.

****

My sister, **Laura Bernice Vinson Freeman** (1904-1995) joined Hopewell Methodist Protestant Church July, 1917, while Rev. W. D. Stewart was pastor. She married Lonnie Freeman on July 17, 1923, and moved her membership soon after to Pierce Chapel Methodist Episcopal Church, where Lonnie was a member. However, they lived near Hopewell for a long time, attended there and most of their children joined Hopewell. Some are still members. Sister was a very determined person. I wondered sometimes if Grandma Ellen Duke Story might have had some similar traits, as her picture seems so. Sister was like Mama. Even when she was in ill health, she kept coming to church. It was an example of faith. She was a very loving mother, grandmother and sister.

****

Mrs. Glennie Horne Herring (1896-1995) lived to be 98. She was a long time member and supporter of Hopewell Church and the women's organizations. She was a lovely, gentle Christian lady. What more can one say?

1 Samuel 3:10b KJV
"Speak: for thy servant heareth."

****

Mrs. Clyde Chadwick Foster (1906-1994) was a member at Hopewell for a long time. She always seemed to be a kind, patient person.

****

Another good friend of mine and an active member of Hopewell Church, **Nellie Mae Gunter Chadwick** (1916-1995), was a past president of the women's organization and a teacher of the Browning Sunday School Class for a number of years. Her husband, Grady, had an extended illness and she was an example of a devoted wife. She was also a loving daughter to her mother, Mayo H. Gunter. Mayo had a lengthy illness and Nellie Mae took care of her.

****

Some older members that I remember by name, but not by face were (including a couple of men here): **Mrs. Fanny Crawford, Mrs. Margaret Taylor McConnell** (1860-1936), **Mr. James L. "Jim" Herring** (1859-1946) and **Mrs. Sarah F. Herring** (1858-1931), **Mr. Jefferson Fletcher Herring** (1872-1942) and **Mrs. Katie Rocquemore Herring** (1875-1963) buried at Watoola UMC. *(Annette's note: I checked on Find-A-Grave and the last two people listed above are the ones buried at Watoola.) (Also, I wonder if the Mrs. Fanny Crawford mentioned here is the wife of the Mr. Crawford Mama mentions in the memories of men. I think so, but I could never find convincing evidence.)*

****

Mrs. Maude Ramsey (1880-1960) joined Hopewell late in her life. However, I heard her say she had been a Christian all her life. She was a genteel lady.

****

Mrs. Minnie R. Foster (1878-1962) always seemed like such a happy person. The main thing I remember about "Mrs. Minnie" was that she always asked to have the pastors to eat dinner (lunch it is now) with them on Monday during revivals in July. The reason she gave was that the iceman brought ice on Monday and they could have iced tea to drink on a hot July day.

****

Mrs. Eulala Riddle Thomas (1877-1953) is listed on the first available membership roll in 1903. It would be so good if earlier membership records had been kept. She married R. R. "Bobbie" Thomas. He helped with the Hopewell Homecoming in 1957. He was a member of a Baptist church, but also supported Hopewell. Their daughter, **Thula Thomas Wilson** (1902-1955), joined Hopewell in 1928. She was a good friend of mine and very active in the Missionary Society. She is buried at Morris Chapel United Methodist Church cemetery.

****

My first memory of Aunt Ethel, **Ethel Deas Story** (1895-1965), was in 1920 at the dining room table at Grandpa and Grandma Story's house. Uncle Alto had just married and brought his tall stately new bride (Will Morrison) to see his family. Aunt Will was "dressed up", probably in her wedding dress. So, Aunt Ethel had "dressed up" in a beautiful dress, which I thought was probably *her* wedding dress. The next time I remember her, she was hand cranking their small two door car. She was teaching school at a school called "The Green School" on the Old Columbus Road near the Union Grove Baptist church. Aunt Ethel had taught school at Hopewell School before she married. After Ellen was born, she did not teach anymore. However, when my brother was in the tenth grade at Opelika Clift High School, he needed some help with English. With knowledge and patience, she helped him to pass his examination. I am sure there were many other times when I was at their house, but the next memory was stopping by their house from school. In 1925, we lived on the Marvyn Road and I rode into Opelika with Miss Lurline Floyd. Each morning I walked from downtown Opelika to Clift High School. After school, I walked back to Aunt Ethel's on 6th Avenue. Uncle Jesse was at work so I didn't see him.

It was in the 1930's when I remember Aunt Ethel being a great leader at Hopewell Church. She taught the Senior Sunday School Class for a long time. She was a leader in the Christian Endeavor and in the Women's Missionary Society. In 1940, after unification, the women's group became known as the Women's Society of Christian Service. On September 7, 1940, Mrs. Jesse Story (Aunt Ethel) was installed as President by Rev. Wilbur Walton, pastor. After Aunt Ethel's health declined and she wasn't able to attend the meeting, she still paid her pledge to missions and I feel sure that she was praying for the group.

After Aunt Ethel was confined to a wheelchair, she could still do many things, including canning pears and cooking. She was a good cook and still invited friends to come eat with them. She was a gracious hostess. After a meal, she did not wash the dishes until after the guests went home. When my mother would go home with Uncle Jesse from church on some Sundays, she would have dinner ready. After a good meal, leisurely eaten, Aunt Ethel would suggest that they go visit a shut-in or someone she thought needed a visit. In 1963, I heard our pastor remark that he went to see "Miss Ethel" to minister to her, but he came away feeling he had been ministered unto. Many others felt that way, too. *(Even as a child, I had the same feeling of being blessed in her presence. aae)*

The most important thing I remember about Aunt Ethel were her prayers. When she bowed her head and closed her eyes in prayer, she seemed so at ease in Her LORD's presence. She gave thanks, asked forgiveness, then asked for blessings for others, her family, and mercy for herself.

I have never been fluent in public prayer as
many people are, so for my pleading,
I am using Romans 8:26 NIV
"In the same way, the Spirit helps us in our weakness.

We do not know what we ought to pray for,
But the Spirit intercedes for us
With groans that words cannot express."
(Thank goodness for this! aae)

****

So far as I know, **Ellen Story Hoople** (1925-1985) is the only "namesake" we have for Ellender Duke Story, who, from our family records, was also called Ellen. When Ellen was very young, she was also very sick. Uncle Jesse and Aunt Ethel carried her to Dr. Dawson in Montgomery, AL. He brought health to their baby and they named her Ellen Dawson Story. Later, Ellen would change her name to Barbara Ellen Story. People at Hopewell always called her Ellen, but others she knew called her Barbara. She is Ellen to me. She was a very smart and energetic child. Aunt Ethel was a good teacher and Ellen probably could read when she started to school. To me, Ellen grew up quickly. When she finished high school at Beauregard, she left home for a job. I don't remember for sure where— maybe New Orleans!! In the 1940's, she came back to Opelika and worked at several places. During this time she met Charles Hoople. He was in the military service on duty guarding German prisoners at the Prison of War Camp in Opelika. I never knew how she met him, nor the details of their marriage. After World War II, Charles remained in the service and they lived in many interesting places around the world. While in Alaska, she sent Annette a pair of mini moccasins. In August, 1962, they had a lovely baby girl named Faith Suzanne. They were very happy and their life changed. In1964, they came to live near Hopewell Church and her parents. By this time, Aunt Ethel's health was in decline. I am sure it made Aunt Ethel happy to have her daughter and her little granddaughter close by. She lovingly cared for her mother. Then, about 1970, when Uncle Jesse began to have health problems, she was near to help care for him.

Ellen became very active in Hopewell Church. She was elected Secretary/ Treasurer in 1965 and served until 1974. She began a campaign to improve the cemetery. A committee consisting of Ellen, her husband Charles, Mrs. Ollie Vinson, Jesse Story, Herron McConnell, and Otis Story was formed to contact families of those buried in the cemetery to get contributions in order to place small markers on all the unmarked graves. (Older people will remember that the unmarked graves were denoted by mounds of dirt, which made it more difficult to care for the cemetery.) She walked the entire cemetery writing names and dates and noting the unmarked graves, creating a record. I am not sure if anyone helped her. Looking back, I am ashamed that I did not. I was probably going to the beauty shop, grocery store, or shelling peas. What were you doing? After the markers were put in place, grass needed to be put out. I remember hearing Otis say that Ellen got so hot helping with the sodding that he sent her home. Again, where was I? Not there.

Ellen and Charles gave a lot of attention to their daughter, Faith. She grew to be one of the most delightful persons I have ever known. Ellen became a member of the United Methodist Women. Charles was elected Sunday School Superintendent one year. I am sure Ellen was pleased that he accepted that role. Ellen loved my mother and gave her special attention. She organized her Aunt Ollie's 83rd birthday party in April, 1967. Her prayers were similar to her mother's for when she prayed, it seemed she was talking to her Creator.

Ellen, Charles, and Faith moved to Columbus, GA, in 1974 to be nearer their work at Fort Benning, GA. That year they gave pew bibles to the church. They continued to support Hopewell financially after they moved to Columbus. After Ellen died in 1985, Charles moved to Atlanta to be near Faith, but he continued to support Hopewell Church financially. Ellen was my relative, my friend and my confidant.

To Ellen:
"Do all the good you can,
By all the means you can,
In all the ways you can,
In all the places you can,
At all the times you can,
To all the people you can,
As long as ever you can."—John Wesley

****

Juanita Parker Freeman (1931-1997) was a faithful and dependable member of Hopewell Church. She went to visit her granddaughter in Smith Station on Sunday February 2, 1997, and never returned home. Her body was found Saturday, March 1, 1997, on the Georgia side of the Chattahoochee River. Juanita, I can't cry enough for the sadness of family and friends in your untimely leaving us.

"...We do not know what tomorrow will bring...." James 4:14 (NRSV)

****

Eula Will Huff Mayberry (1927-) started bringing her little girls, Becky and Kathy, to Sunday School in 1958. She was the Kindergarten Assistant Teacher. My mother, known to Eula Will as Miss Ollie, was the teacher. She was very fond of Eula Will. When my mother retired from teaching Sunday School, Eula Will saw that she received several nice gifts from the Sunday School and the Church. For the many services that Eula Will has given to Hopewell United Methodist Church, we want her to know how much we appreciate her service and that of Becky and Kathy.

Eula Will is my friend and she is
"As constant as the Northern Star
And as bright and shining as the morning star."

****

I had the great fortune of working side-by-side with my wonderful friend, **Mrs. Jewel Herring Clegg** (1922-2009) for many years at the Agricultural Stabilization and Conservation Service in Opelika. She was a wonderful co-worker. She and her husband, Walter Clegg, were also wonderful members of Hopewell Church. They were faithful in attendance and financially. Jewel was a member of the women's group from the time she joined the church. They brought their daughter, Linda, to church and Sunday School. I am proud to have been her friend.

****

Margie McConnell Mullins (1930-1998), along with her family, was a friendly and faithful member at Hopewell Church. She brought up her sons to be Godly men. They still attend church today.

****

Mrs. Carolyn B. McConnell (1945-) joined our church soon after she married Jack McConnell. She has been an inspiration to us all as she has been very active in all phases of our church ministry. She was totally responsible for the Circuit-wide event, "Sweet Tea and Jesus", held at Hopewell starting in 2006.

****

Hopewell Women Mentioned

By Estelle Allen

Mrs. Emma Irene Jones Allen – 1869-1925
Mrs. Fannie Story Browning – 1853-1922
Mrs. Nellie Mae Gunter Chadwick – 1916-1995
Mrs. Jewel Herring Clegg – 1922-2009
Mrs. Ruth Murphree Dorsey – 1906-1974
Miss Alma Foster – 1902-1944
Mrs. Clyde Chadwick Foster – 1906-1994
Mrs. Minnie Ramsey Foster -1878-1962
Mrs. Laura Bernice Vinson Freeman – 1904-1995
Mrs. Juanita Parker Freeman – 1931-1997
Mrs. Glennie Horne Herring – 1896-1995
Mr. James L (1859-1946) and Mrs. Sarah F Herring- 1858-1931
Mr. Jefferson Fletcher (1872-1942) and Mrs. Katie Rocquemore Herring – 1875-1963
Mrs. Sara Allen Hinson – 1909-1985

Mrs. Barbara Ellen Story Hoople – 1925-1985

Mrs. Antionette (Nettie) Story Jones – 1845-1927

Mrs. Eula Will Huff Mayberry- 1927-

Mrs. Carolyn B. McConnell - 1945-

Mrs. Margaret Taylor McConnell – 1860-1936

Miss Frances Meadows – 1921-1981

Mrs. Gemmie Browning Meadows – 1887-1956

Mrs. Margie McConnell Mullins – 1930-1998

Mrs. Evanelle Story Porch – 1925-1988

Mrs. Maude Ramsey – 1880-1960

Mrs. Louise Ramsey Roberts – 1909-1988

Mrs. Willie V. Littleton Rudd – 1895-1956 and Mr. Anson Rudd

Mrs. Ethel Deas Story – 1895-1965

Miss Leonora Louanna Story – 1850-1934

Mrs. Lillie Thomas Story – 1902-1989

Mrs. Mary Virginia Allen Story – 1914-1987

Miss Mildred V. Story – 1908-1976

Mrs. Sultana Elizabeth Cadenhead Story – 1857-1953

Mrs. Eulala Riddle Thomas – 1877-1953

Miss Sammie Ramsey Tinsley– 1890-1969

Mrs. Agnes Howard Vinson – 1918-1983

Mrs. Laura Olivia Story Vinson – 1884-1980

Mrs. Esther Lynch Whatley -1873-1950

Mrs. Willie Hinson Widener - 1903-1985

Mrs. Thula Beatrice Thomas Wilson – 1902-1955

Mrs. Betty Word – 1869-1951

Note: There are three men listed here as they are spoken about in the memories of women.

(The following is a letter written by Estelle Allen in 1997)
Memories

4292 Alabama Highway 169
Opelika, AL 36804

Dear

In 1995, while recuperating in a nursing home, there came into my heart a longing to collect memories of Hopewell Church and get them published.

At home in 1996, this desire did not wane, so I sent out a letter to many of you. Now it is 1997 and I am disappointed in how few responses I have received. However, I am very touched by the content of the memories I have gotten.

These memories range from about the old singing, shouting church to our modern one. They include memories of people, pastors, revivals, weddings, reunnions, events, programs, the building, the cemetary and "dinner on the ground".

They came from a diverse group. Some that have lived a lifetime nearby, some who lived here in their youth only, others with ancestral connections only. Some are long and some are short.

To most of you, this is not your first notice. I would very much like for you to have a part in the Book of Memories and History of Hopewell United Methodist Church. I look forward to receiving your memories soon!

With love and best wishes,

Mrs. Leon Allen

"Memories grow more meaningful with every passing year,
More precious and more beautiful, more treasured and more dear."
by Helen Steiner Rice

Memories Submitted by Friends and Family Members

Memories of Hopewell Church

L. H. Allen, Jr.
December 22, 1996

GOING TO CHURCH

I remember going to church one day soon after some road work had been done to shape the road bank in front of the building. As we rounded the bend, my father noticed the good work that had been done. I noticed the fresh new bank of earth and thought it looked so nice and tall (to a very young child). Erosion has not been a problem; the earthen bank stands today much as it did then. Of course, now we have brick steps and a brick walkway from the road level up to the steps of the church.

Sunday morning was always a busy time at home: getting breakfast, reading Sunday School lessons, taking baths, etc. However, often there was still enough time for my father and me to take walks around the property, particularly in the pasture or woods. My father would always talk about things he would like to do; improvements in the pasture, trees that could be cut soon for lumber of for pulpwood, and draining and clearing the bottom land for drought-free pasture. The land was never drained. Instead a community of beavers moved in and flooded much of the area. I was always glad that the bottom land was never cleared. Today it would fall into a "wetlands" category and it would be hard to change its condition from tree swamp to drained pasture land. One day I flew over the area with Donald Duffey and got a good look at the work of the beaver colony.

But I digress! My father and I always got back to the house in time to get ready to go to church. We always arrived at church promptly every Sunday; exactly at 10:10 A.M. for the 10:00 A.M. opening service! We were never late!

THE BUILDING

I don't need to describe the building for those who know it well presently, but maybe for the future. Hopewell Church had a much higher ceiling than most local churches. It had creaky wooden floors, a fancy double-grooved tongue-in-groove ceiling (and maybe walls, too). I looked at the ceiling a lot under two circumstances: (1) fire and brimstone sermons, and (2) paper wasps circling the ceiling after being warmed up by the wood stove heater.

Ah! The wood stove heater. I remember more about it on cold winter Sunday evenings than any other time. We first came to Sunday evening (night) meetings to attend Christian Endeavor. Later our congregation was modernized with the advent of Methodist Youth Fellowship (MYF).

The wood burning heater was started with a kindling wood of heartwood pine (chock full of natural combustible resins put on earth to enable people to start their fires to stave off hypothermia). This kindling wood was given a name (most likely the original name degenerated) that cannot be spelled using the standard twenty six letters of the English alphabet. It is probably a primary example of the regression of language from a crisp enunciation backward toward primeval grunts and simple utterances. Enough already!

The kindling wood was called light'od. (Momma says it came from light wood, which came maybe from lighting wood, as in to light a fire.) I think it was sometimes called fat light'od or fat pine light'od.

After the wood burning heater was loaded with light'od and fuel wood, the light'od was ignited with a match and before long the heater was warm and toasty. I am certain that an energy budget analysis would show that most of the heat was conveyed up the metal pipe chimney to the firebrick chimney and back to the ambient environment, with much of the original input gases being replaced by fresh air flowing in from outside! Nevertheless, we had no excess carbon monoxide or carbon dioxide problems with this system!

The stove would sometimes get so hot that the metal pipe would glow red right above the stove, and sometimes the stove walls themselves would glow red. I liked to stare at the warm, red surface. The radiant energy from the glowing wood stove kept us warm enough for the duration of MYF. I don't remember much about the convective heat. Since warm air is displaced by more dense cold air, I suppose it was pushed up to the 14-foot high ceiling, while our feet endured the fresh supply of outside air that clung along the floor.

The outside of the church sanctuary was painted white. The roof was composed of wooden shingles. These had to be fat pine shingles to survive the humid environment of the Southeast. Later on, the roof was replaced with asphalt shingles.

When I was in my very early teens (or late preteens), the elders and officials of the church decided to build Sunday School rooms. Before that time, two groups of the smallest children were taught behind two Z-fold solid green screens at the back corners of the church. They were the Beginner's and Primary Classes, I think.

I remember helping with building the north wing Sunday School rooms. They were built largely on Saturdays by the congregation with Uncle Jesse Story taking the lead, since he was a carpenter by profession.

One frigid Saturday afternoon, Marion Story (Uncle Jesse's son) came riding up from his house about a mile away, bareback on a red mule. The significant part of this story is that Marion was not only riding barebacked on the mule, but he was also riding barefoot in the freezing weather. I don't know what the significance is of this significant part of the story. I leave that up to the reader to contemplate.

The first part of building the Sunday School rooms was to calculate the height of the concrete block pillars to support the floor joists, subflooring and floor to make the floor level with the existing floor of the main building. Calculations were made, footings poured, concrete block pillars laid, framing for floor joists mounted and nailed in place, and the subflooring nailed down. Then it was discovered that he top of the subflooring was at the same level as the finished floor of the main church. Or maybe it was later when they cut the door (or opened the already finished door).

Uncle Jesse always had words for such occasions as these. He would say simply "Bow-wow, wow!" several times, sometimes repeated occasionally over the next ten or twenty minutes.

At any rate, nobody got it right, because I remember that this decision of the height of the pillars was arrived at by church committee, after a little measuring and much discussion among the adults.

Today, after installation of thick, luxuriant carpeting in the altar area of the Sanctuary, and maybe after re-flooring, the height of the two floors seemed to match exactly. Maybe there was a long term reason for a short term shortfall.

THE GROUNDS

I think we should start with geology here, because background and underpinning influence much of human status and behavior without us really understanding the roots of things beyond the concepts that occurred when we first became remembering and thinking beings, usually sometimes in childhood, if at all.

Hopewell Church was built along a relatively high ridge at the northern fringe of the Coastal Plains Physiographic Province. The soils are deep and sandy, and often permeated with small, rounded marine-washed stones of about one to two inches in diameter. The Piedmont Plateau lies to the north, but this geologic discontinuity is separated (locally) by Flake Creek. It has often puzzled me why the Coastal Plains ridge lies at a higher elevation than the southernmost fringes of the Piedmont Plateau. I have figured out a reason, can you? The sandy ridge appears to be related to a ridge that extends from Virginia to Alabama, and is most prominent in South Carolina, Georgia, and North Carolina. These soils are deep, sandy and usually infertile. They seem to support black jack oak and off-type hickory rather than native vegetation indicative of more fertile sites in the area.

The Church has had quarterly meetings, reunions, and other occasions which have led to dinner-on-the-grounds. The geology has conspired to provide two hazards beyond the usual complement of houseflies, ants, gnats (the flying eye, ear, nose, and throat scourge), excess sun (or electricity or hydrometers). These two hazards are spherical and about one inch in diameter; namely small rocks and the numerous hickory nuts produced on trees by the dinner-on-the-grounds table. (A lesser hazard is acorns produced by the black jack oak.) Have you ever witnessed a lady walking across the grounds carrying a container of food in both hands and stepping daintily and ladylike across a carpet of unyielding quartz stones, hickory nuts, and black jack oak acorns? The accomplished foot work is more like birling than modeling. Maybe it should be an Olympic event!

Oh, by the way, I was very surprised one day decades later to discover that there is a vegetative creeping colony of cactus (looks like a member of the genus *Opuntia*) spreading across the cemetery. I am sure that it still exists, unless extraordinary steps have been taken to eradicate it.

As a child, I remember walking through the cemetery many times. I thought some of the markers (slabs) were extremely old, although many had been placed relatively recently. One of the things I remember was Aunt Ethel Deas Story discussing the relative beauty of marble markers with respect to granite markers. She liked the marble better. They were nice and white with "marbling" streaks and patterns of gray and black inclusions in the material.

My, but times have changed. Aunt Ethel was a very observant, intelligent lady and I am sure that her observations and opinion would have changed too. Lo and behold, marble does not withstand weathering as well as granite. Most of the marble markers are now stained with age, whereas the granite stones remain relatively unscathed. Apparently, not only does marble weather chemically, but also biologically. Small organisms can penetrate the small cracks of the crystal structure and promote further dissolution of the calcium carbonate. Furthermore, at least one marble marker has developed a long cleavage in the rock, probably as a result of the external forces that kneaded and metamorphosed the original limestone source material.

SUNDAY SCHOOL

I am not certain that I can remember all my Sunday School teachers. One, of course, was my grandmother, Olivia Story Vinson. The reader can learn much more about her in the book, "We Remember the Best—A Collection of Memories and a Tribute to Laura Olivia Story Vinson".

Sunday School was held under various conditions, first behind folded room dividers in the main church sanctuary. Later Sunday School was held in the north side Sunday School rooms. Eventually, the teens met in the fellowship Hall. I do not remember exactly when the Fellowship Hall was built, probably after I moved away from home. *(Editor's note: The Fellowship Hall was built in 1964.)*

I remember Aunt Ethel Deas Story best as a Sunday School teacher. Aunt Ethel had knowledge of the Scriptures beyond that strictly written in the Bible. She had attended a college sometime earlier in life. At any rate, she provided much history, insight and integration of the whole message of the Scriptures. I think I had been exposed to the clustering of the books of the Bible. The Pentateuch, The Prophets, The Gospels, The Epistles, The Revelation, etc., at some time earlier but Aunt Ethel helped put meaning into this classification.

Editor's Note: The following outline is probably what Hartwell was referring to:

THE OLD TESTAMENT
The Pentateuch (first five books, also called The Law)
Historical (Joshua – Nehemiah)
Wisdom (or Poetic Writings) (Job – Song of Solomon)
Major Prophets (Isaiah – Ezekiel)
Minor Prophets (Daniel – Malachi)
THE NEW TESTAMENT
The Gospels (Matthew – John)
The Acts of the Apostles
The Letters of Paul (Romans – Hebrews)
The Epistles (James – Jude)
The Revelation

Sunday School would always be preceded by an opening service of song, Bible reading, commentary, and prayer led by the Sunday School Superintendent. Those I remember best were my Grandmother Vinson, Uncle Jesse Story, and my father.

THE MINISTERS

Apparently, the earliest minister that I should have remembered was Brother Wilbur Walton, but I actually do not remember him. However, he seemed to have set the standard by which every succeeding minister was judged (evaluated) by the elders of the church. (These "elders" I was later to realize were actually middle-aged people rather than truly senior citizens.) I will use another written record to establish the chronology of these ministers' service in the Lee Circuit and at Hopewell.

Rev. Wilbur Walton – 1936 –

Rev. T. H. Maxey – 1942 -. I only remember when the new minister came.

Rev. Kelly Scott – 1943 -. I remember when he replaced Maxey.

Rev. Robert Wilson – 1945 -. This is the first minister that I remember distinctly. He was a young, vibrant active man with a clear, loud (not raucous) delivery who could really inspire the congregation. Brother

Wilson also taught at Beauregard High School, so we saw him during the week as well as on Sundays. I remember him well for his efforts in leading Pine Grove Church to build a new building. One day I saw him in overalls on a ladder painting the outside of the new building as it was being completed.

Rev. H. F. Wesley – 1948 -. Brother Wesley was already an elderly man when he and his wife came to the circuit. He was fond of punctuating his sermons by addressing us as "… Brothers, Sisters, friends…"

Rev. Carl Williams – 1950 -. This minister seemed to think of himself as sort of an intellectual or an "avant-garde" person, and maybe he was. I remember once he preached a whole sermon asking the congregation what he should preach. I must have been fourteen, going on fifteen, when he arrived, so I was already largely capable of comprehending adults at any level by that time. I remember some heated discussion by some adults about his style, content, and delivery. One person declared that he should "PREACH THE GOSPEL". I always felt that Carl Williams got a bum rap from the congregation as a whole. Maybe he deserved it, maybe he did not. Maybe he did not really comprehend his congregation. I really cannot remember if Carl Williams was a proponent of what might have been called "the social gospel" in contrast to "the individual gospel".

Dropping back in time, I remember that Robert Wilson once delivered a sermon describing worship and service to God. He said that some people believed in a "shouting" religion, some in a "singing" religion and others in various other forms of expression in worship. But Brother Wilson said that he believed in an "action" religion. I think he realized that commitment was the bottom-line component of religion. And I think that he believed that the social gospel was one element of this commitment.

Rev. Glenn Sirmon – 1951 -. Glenn Sirmon was a seriously dedicated young man still showing a lot of elements of youthful exuberance and patterns of young adult behavior. I remember him best for taking a number of us to a retreat at Blue Lake in South Alabama. His wife was an excellent piano player.

Rev. James Love – 1954 -. Rev. Love was a levelheaded, relatively soft-spoken minister.

Rev. Charles Pittman – 1955. Charles Pittman was another young man very much interested in the youth of the church.

I will stop my commentary about ministers here. In 1958, Rev. Gillis Crenshaw came to Lee Circuit and I left for Cornell University. I lived in Opelika again for a short period while Rev. R. C. Warren was on the Lee Circuit in 1962.

MYF

Actually, I think I enjoyed MYF as much as any aspect of church. We often had meetings with other groups in the Opelika area. One especially important person in MYF was the youth services leader at the First Methodist Church in Opelika, Mary Elsie Laurence. She was the daughter of Rev. R. I. Laurence and Mrs. Laurence, who had a large family of sons and daughters. Mary Elsie was committed to leadership of the younger generation of her time.

IN CONCLUSION

Much of this narrative is written from memory, which reminds me of my favorite quotation, paraphrased below:

"The faintest ink is clearer than the best memory."
B. Franklin

Among modern humanity, at least, only that which is preserved in writing will be passed along. Talk is cheap and fleeting. Stone is better than wood; granite is better than marble (in most cases.)

****

Dorothy Hinson Bell (1934-2008)

I remember the Christmas plays we always had at Christmas. We put a wire across the front of the church and pinned white sheets across for the curtains. I remember how Mama always sat at the same place every time we went to church. We went to church almost every Sunday. After Ralph and I married, Ed, our son, always looked forward to coming to Sunday School and seeing Cousin Ollie. He liked to sing the songs that she taught him in the Kindergarten Class. Ed also liked to come to Bible School. He especially liked the craft classes and still has a cross that he made when he was a young boy.

****

Dorothy Story Blackburn (1927-2006)

Estelle, you asked about memories of Hopewell. I'm sure Charles would have had many great memories, but a few have stayed with me my lifetime. Mostly, I guess, in the 1930's, it was always a great place to meet the many cousins. I remember all the great food on days when dinner on the grounds was served, especially Aunt Ethel Story's "checkered chocolate and white cake". Another memory I have is of seeing communion being received from a common cup. Growing up in the city where we never had food outside or the one communion cup both left lifetime impressions on me.

*(I also remember Aunt Ethel Story's checkerboard
cake. Probably where I got the idea I wanted
some of those pans. Well, I have some. I've made
some cakes, but am now too lazy.) Estelle*

****

I Remember Hopewell

Some of my earliest memories include visits to Hopewell Church. Among them are included what were called "Quarterly Meetings". I had little understanding of the real purpose of these gatherings which included "dinner-on-the-grounds". We all gathered around a picnic style feast under the trees after the morning service. Long tables were burdened with the best foods from the best cooks in the community. The luscious layer cake that Cousin Ethel Story always brought was a great piece de resistance. It was somehow arranged to make a checkerboard design. My second dessert was a piece of sweet potato pie that Cousin Ollie Vinson usually had— so good! My mother filled her basket with baked chicken and dressing or barbecued chicken and potato salad. The lemon cheese cake that was a specialty of my older sister, Lucy, completed the basket meal. We children always hoped there would be some left to take back home. After the dinner, the officials convened to attend to the business of the church.

Frequent visits to the nearby cemetery where many of my relatives were buried was always interesting. The exact relationship of the occupant of each grave was recited by an older member of the family. The large tomb above the ground that was sheltered with a gazebo-like cover had an interesting history, though exact details have escaped me.

The Christmas programs on the Sunday night before Christmas were warmed by the potbellied stove. Cousin Jesse Story was the chief "stoker of the fire" until Leon Allen inherited that job. Together, they managed to keep us warm, though there were times that we kept on our coats! After the pageant portraying the nativity story, which was usually produced and directed by Estelle Allen, we exchanged inexpensive gifts.

My earliest memory of a church service there was led by the pastor we called Brother Conner. The music was led by Miss Alma Foster at the pump organ and Mr. Jim Tom McConnell directing the singing. Later when a piano was used at the worship service, Mildred Story was the pianist. My sister, Frances, played at times. I think she might have been a substitute.

Young members of the church families were some of my best friends; many were relatives. We often exchanged "all day" visits on Sundays from noon through dinner until Christian Endeavor time on Sunday evenings.

I witnessed firsthand part of the actual construction of the "new" church. I was allowed to "tag along" when my parents went by to observe the progress of the carpenters.

It was much later in my life that I realized that my relationship with Hopewell Church would become very influential in my life. For this, I am very grateful.

Hazel Meadows Calhoun (1919-2009)

****

I joined Hopewell church when I was 17 years old (July, 1934) during a revival meeting. I was never active at Hopewell, but did enjoy visiting there. As you know I grew up in the Pierce Chapel Methodist Church. My older brother and sisters all attended and joined Pierce Chapel because it was in walking distance of our home. My brother, Vernon, joined at Mt. Olive Baptist Church where my father, Charlie Whatley, was a member. When I was very young I wanted to join at Pierce Chapel and Mama wanted me to wait until I was older. At the time I joined Hopewell, Pierce Chapel was not as strong a church as Hopewell because of the depression, I think. There was talk of combining the two churches. I attended Hopewell off and on with my Mama, Esther Lynch Whatley, as a child and always enjoyed going. The main memory I have is that we always went into the cemetery and Mama pointed out the graves of our Lynch relatives. That was very interesting to me. Another fond memory was that Mr. and Mrs. John Allen always invited us home with them for Sunday dinner. They always had a delicious meal although they did not know that we would be there that Sunday. What fascinated me was their round dinner table with a lazy susan on it and the way it was turned around for us to help our plates. I always wanted a table like that. In 1961, I had a table with a lazy susan built with six Captain and mate chairs. I had it handmade out of maple. I gave this table to my adopted daughter, Patricia, for her home before I moved from North Carolina to Louisiana in 1980.

I enjoyed hearing Mama tell about driving the buggy back to Hopewell to church when my older brothers and sisters were little. She would have 4 or 5 children in the buggy at a time. What an effort that must have been getting her and the children all "dressed up" after doing all her household chores on the farm! Papa helped her some with the chores. He was a strong Baptist, but it was never a source of friction in our home.

I have some good memories of some of my Lynch relatives. I remember when Uncle Arthur Lynch came to see us. We were happy to see him; he was so jolly and pleasant and full of life. So were Uncle Kim Lynch and his son, Gladys. They all had a contagious laugh that always spread to others. When Uncle Arthur would come to spend the night, Mama would get our family Bible at bedtime and give it to him to read. After he read some in it, he would get on his knees in front of his chair and all of us would do the same. He would pray sincerely. I remember my sister, Ethel, saying that she always felt close to heaven at those times. I can say the same thing. To quote Valerie, she wrote in our "family book", "These were sacred occasions for us, a time when we felt as one in the spirit as a family, and together in communion with God." Valerie wrote that we also had Bible reading and prayer the same way when Uncle Kim and Grandpa William Lynch came to visit. "Grandma Frances Bentley Lynch", wrote Valerie, "liked to quote Bible verses and taught her and Mama many of them." Great-great grandfather Bentley was a Methodist minister, but I don't know if he ever went to Hopewell or not. Both of my grandparents on my mother's side did, I'm sure.

I remember "Miss" Ollie Vinson quite well. She was one of Mama's best friends at Hopewell.

Violet Whatley Dorsett

(I remember hearing Daddy talk about the round table with the lazy susan at his parents' home.) AAE

****

When I was five to eight or nine years old, we went to Sunday School and Church on Sunday. Sometimes my daddy (Lonnie Freeman) would go and sometimes it was just me, my mama (Bernice Freeman), my sister and my two brothers who would go. As long as we were in Grandma Vinson's Sunday School class, we were pretty good. But, generally, my brother Billy, my nephew Sonny and I were "kinda" aggravating kids. In other classes, we would talk, laugh, hide, even jump out the window! We got several whippings before we decided to be "good". I also remember going to Bible School nearly every summer. This was lots of fun. We studied the Bible, played games, made crafts, and even had Grandma's famous tea cakes for refreshments some days. I went to church some after I was grown, but not as much as I should have. The church brings lots of good memories and a few sad ones, but if there's a church I call my own, it is Hopewell United Methodist. I learned a lot there.

Shirley Freeman Downs

****

We got married at Hopewell Church on December 31, 1987. It was Don's idea. He has always liked that church. Charles Hoople walked me down the aisle. My mother-in-law, Annette Edwards, Grandma Allen, and Lenora Allen did a terrific job with the church decorating. Some churches do not allow videotaping, but Pastor Charles Knight allowed it. It is great having everything on tape. The ceremony was beautiful. People came from all over. My mom, Margit Goettling, came from Germany. My uncle and aunt came from Canada. Don's mom came from South Carolina, Don's Aunt Lenora from Georgia, my sister-in-law, Lauren, from New Jersey, Don's Uncle Hartwell from Florida, and others from Huntsville, Alabama, where we live. Don's other sisters, Alicia and Maria, did a great job helping out. Don, Sr., Walter Duffey, and Charles Hoople videotaped. Chris Goggans lit the candles. After the wedding we all went to Grandma Allen's and opened presents. I married into a wonderful family. I have lost both of my grandparents. It is great having another grandmother. She is great!!

Karin Goettling-Duffey
Wife of Don Duffey, Jr.
Karin had asked to have a German chocolate
cake for the reception. She had one.
(Grandma Allen)

****

The Little White Church On The Hill

Now known as Hopewell United Methodist Church
by Annette Allen Edwards

I used to love the song "The Church in the Wildwood". Even though it is about a little brown church in a valley, I always related it to my little white church on the hill, HOPEWELL. Hearing that song has always brought a feeling of warmth to me.

My memories of Hopewell Methodist Church are so closely entwined with my memories of my family that it is hard to separate the two. I begin with thoughts of taking part in programs at the front of the church when I was in my grandmother's Beginners Sunday School Class and the evening meeting called The Christian Endeavor, as it was called at the time. As a group, the Beginner's Class would sing little songs we had learned in our class in front of the congregation on special occasions, such as Easter Sunday and Christmas. Among my favorites were "Jesus Loves Me", "Praise Him, Praise Him", and "Jesus Loves the Little Children". Grandma would teach us new songs from time to time, but the old standbys were always my favorites. I loved "Away In A Manger" at Christmastime, but it was always hard for me to sing. Often we were given little poems or Scripture verses to recite. I don't remember any of them now, but I always thought being "on the program" was great fun. I remember the first time I read a passage of Scripture at the evening meeting; my mother had to assure all the adults that I was really reading and had not memorized the passage.

She had made me practice reading at home many times in preparation, but I was really reading at the age of four. I learned to read at my grandmother's side while she listened and helped my brother with his reading lessons.

An early memory that comes to mind is that of planning to join the church at the Revival when I was five years old. I sat with a group of young people, including my brother, who were planning to join the church at the end of the sermon on Friday night, the last night of the Revival. To make a long story short, I fell asleep and the service went on without my participation. I was very disappointed. My mother said that I must not be old enough to join and insisted that I wait until the following year's Revival to join.

This experience brings to mind another "sleep experience". There was a wiener roast planned, complete with bonfire, for a Saturday night at the church. I was so excited. It seems we were at Grandma Story's and you guessed it, I went to sleep before it was time to leave for the event. Mama left me at Grandma's while the rest of the family went to the wiener roast. I was so mad at Mama. It took me a long time to get over that!

Other than family gatherings, Hopewell Methodist Church and the activities there were almost exclusively the social life of our family when I was very small, and continued to be a large part of our social life through my high school years. As a child, I thought there could not be a service at the church unless my parents were there to open the church doors. There was Sunday School every Sunday morning and Christian Endeavor (later MYF) every Sunday night, Sunday morning and evening worship services once a month when I was young. From time to time over the years, there were Wednesday night prayer meetings and the occasional choir practice. Ever since I can remember, the ladies of the church met one Saturday afternoon a month. The group was called the Women's Society of Christian Service. We called it the "women's society meeting". Later it was named The Women's Society of Missionary Service, and we called it the "missionary meeting". Some of these were held at different members' homes. Some were held at the church. When I was young, these women brought their children to the meetings and one of their group was in charge of the "children's group". I remember these meetings as my first touch with the idea of missions and of learning about foreign cultures. Often a good bit of time was spent playing games. One I remember playing when my grandmother was the children's leader was "Drop the Handkerchief".

When I was a little girl, I remember wanting to sit with some of the other children during church services, but my mother would insist that I sit with her. She did not want me causing a disturbance and her being unable to reach over and pinch me! At least that's what I thought!

During the years of my earliest memories, Hopewell was part of a five-church charge called the Lee Circuit. The other churches were Pine Grove, Beulah, Pierce Chapel, and Morris Chapel. As I write this, Pierce Chapel, Morris Chapel, and Hopewell make up a three-church charge. Every quarter, there was a fifth Sunday in a month and a quarterly conference was held at one of the churches, alternately. We were always there. I enjoyed these meetings, because you got to see so many people from the other churches. There was always "dinner on the grounds". We called it the "quarterly meeting".

Revivals were always exciting to me. Usually the ministers were previous favorite preachers. A favorite of mine was Rev. Robert Wilson. He was called back to lead revivals at least two times. Lots of people who did not normally come to our church came to the meetings. Many of them were from our church charge. Perhaps they came to hear their favorite past pastors. Maybe they came to support other churches on the charge. Maybe they came for the music. We always had lots of singing of old revival type songs, and when we had a good pianist, the piano would really bounce. I played the piano for a number of years and most people seemed to like my chord-style. Actually I learned that style from the wife of a former pastor, Thelma Sirmon. She played the piano with wild abandon and I loved it. She was probably my favorite preacher's wife. She was young and pretty and I naively thought she picked me out specially to be my friend!

We used to have what were called "Socials" designed especially for the youth. Believe it or not, the young people would come and we would play games. My mother had a couple of "game books" from which she would glean interesting things for us to do. Our Halloween event was Trick or Treat for UNICEF. We did not dress up as ghouls and ghosts and go house to house for candy. We did have occasional hay rides in the fall. That was always fun. We sometimes went caroling at Christmas time and had special Christmas presentations at the church.

Once we had a Rice Supper. Everyone ate rice prepared by ladies of the church and all donated the money they would have spent on dinner that night to missions.

Before an air conditioner was put in, we used funeral home supplied paper fans. In the summer, I suppose the doors and windows were left open for ventilation, but that only meant lots of wasps flying about. Sometimes, the fans were used to swat a wasp or two.

There were three funerals held at Hopewell that affected me greatly when I was growing up. My grandfather, whom I called Papa, died when I was 10 years old. That entire period was probably the most traumatic of my young life. Next, I remember when my cousin's son, Jimmy Howard, was buried at Hopewell. He was perhaps the youngest family member that I remember dying as a youth. Later, on my daddy's birthday in 1955, my boyfriend, Emmett Poulas, was in a wreck and died a few days later. This is spoken about in more detail in my mother's memories of men. Because it was Daddy's birthday, I had gone home with my family instead of spending Sunday afternoon with Emmett. Otherwise I would have been in that wreck too. The two more recent funerals that still weigh heavily on my mind are my mother's, Estelle Vinson Allen (1909-2010), and my daughter's, Lauren Duffey Dempsey(1962-2010). Mama died November 7th and was buried November 11, 2010. Lauren died exactly one month later and her cremains were placed in the gravesite beside my mother's grave on December 11, 2010.

****

Kelly and Margaret Freeman

Kelly attended Hopewell Church as a child. He especially remembers the quarterly meetings because of all the good food. He can still see the tables of delicious food and desserts that will make your mouth water even years and years later. Kelly can remember walking through the woods from the old Davis place over to Grandma and Grandpa Vinson's house and walking down the hill to Hopewell Church. Kelly also reflects on one of his favorite pastors, Robert Wilson, and how much of an influence he had on his life. Kelly also attended classes at Beauregard School taught by Pastor Wilson. Kelly and Margaret were married by Pastor Wesley at the parsonage on July 23, 1949. Margaret moved her membership to Hopewell shortly thereafter. One of Margaret's favorite memories was the Sunday School class they attended. Aunt Ethel Story was the teacher and we loved her dearly. We still have a Bible that the Sunday School class gave us for a wedding gift. The people in our class at that time were: Dorothy Hinson, Bobby Story, Ramona Dunn, G. L. Story, Cynthia Dunn, Tommy Nixon, Marie Hinson, Wayne Freeman, Juanita Freeman and Mrs. Eugene Roberts, our teacher. Although we moved away and moved our membership, Hopewell and the many people we were associated with have always been special to us. Since our retirement, we have moved our membership back to Hopewell. We are not able to attend services as regularly as we would like, but our prayers and support are always there.

****

Kathy Glover

I don't know exactly where to start. Maybe at the beginning would be a good place. I came to Hopewell when I was a toddler, although I don't have any memories of those early years. Just the ones told to me by my mother of the many "switchings" I got for misbehaving in church. I guess those were not good memories for me—that's why I don't remember them. My first memories are those from Bible School and Sunday School and a wonderful lady named Miss Ollie. I remember her pleasant smile and singing all the choruses—"Jesus Love Me", "Jesus Loves All the Little Children", "Deep and Wide"... I remember my mother going over to Mrs. Barbara Chandler's house to plan for Bible School. I remember playing "rock school" on the steps in front of the church, the Kool-Aid and cookies (yum, yum!) Other Sunday School teachers that I remember are Mrs. Estelle Allen, Mrs. Ellen Hoople, and Mrs. Agnes Vinson.

I remember days before we had air conditioning, fanning with those paper fans, the old benches with wooden slats and no cushions. I remember all the "new" preachers and revivals when the preacher would eat at different houses with families. That was a very special time when my mother and grandmother would prepare the "perfect" meal and we would get to eat out of the fancy dishes and drink out of those pretty green iced tea glasses.

In my teenage years, I remember UMYF with Pierce Chapel. Lots of Sunday nights after church we would go out to eat. Those were some of the best times of my life. We would laugh so much! Some of my favorite pastors during this time were Phillip Craddock, Phillip McVay, and Judd Stinson. One time when Judd was our pastor, our youth group went ice skating. That was the first and only time I have ever been. I could not stay on my feet. By the time we left, my clothes were soaked from falling on the ice.

When I was about 16 years old, I remember coming to church one Sunday and our pianist, Mrs. Ruth Dorsey, never showed up. This was not like her, so after church some men from the church went to her house to see if something was wrong. They never found Mrs. Dorsey. Our church was without a pianist. I began playing. At first I had a list of songs that I could play. We had to sing these same songs over and over every Sunday. As I learned more, I added them to my list. I still cannot play every song in the hymnal, but I can play a lot more than I could 24 years ago! I remember Mrs. Eugene Roberts slipping a $5.00 bill in my hand one Sunday and telling me it was for playing the piano.

I remember all the special people that I would not have known if I was not a part of Hopewell Church. I still miss many of those that have passed on, such as Mr. and Mrs. Otis Story, Mr. and Mrs. Eugene Roberts, Mrs. Bernice Freeman, Mrs. Ollie Vinson and Mr. Walter Clegg.

In 1983, I was married at Hopewell. In 1986, my first daughter, Joni, was christened by Rev. Andy Knight. I have lots of fond memories of Andy and his family. In 1991, my youngest daughter, Kaley, was christened on Mother's Day. This was a very special Mother's Day for me. I also remember Joni singing her first solo in church when she was about 5 years old.

I have been teaching first grade for 16 years at Beauregard Elementary School and this year I have a little girl name Olivia Wise. Another teacher remarked one day that she like Olivia's name. I shared with this teacher that Olivia was named after her great- great grandmother and how I called her great-great grandmother "Miss Ollie". I am very grateful to have known Olivia's great-great grandmother and her great grandmother, Mrs. Estelle Allen. This is the first time this has happened in my 16 years of teaching. (Sadly, I hardly even know the mother of some of my students.)

I remember "Miss Ollie" sitting in her wheel chair, hardly ever missing a Sunday and not even being able to hear what the preacher was saying. Many years later, I remember "Miss Bernice" Freeman sitting in her wheelchair in the same spot as her mother had. I remember the handshakes and neck hugs each Sunday from both of these special ladies. Their presence each Sunday was a witness to me.

Another special lady that has been a blessing to Hopewell Church and continues to be a blessing today is Mrs. Estelle Allen. Three words come to mind to describe her—An Amazing Lady!

I remember Mr. Leon Allen when he was our Sunday School Superintendent almost always ending his prayers with "forgive us of our sins and accept our thanks. Amen".

****

From Melissa Pate Hearn

When I was a girl about 8 to 10 years old, my mother, Bobbie Hightower Pate, and I lived near Hopewell church. Mr. and Mrs. Charles Hoople lived on the other side of us. They had a daughter, Faith, who was about my age. We were good pals. They would often pick me up and take me to church.

The most outstanding memory was the singing of the good "ole songs". Everyone was always glad to see you on a Sunday morning. Sunday dinner on the grounds and Revival services there were always great. Being there recently at my Aunt Sara's funeral brought back wonderful feelings and memories of Hopewell Church and its people.

I remember seeing Mr. Burns put Vick's salve in his mouth before singing a solo. One special song I remember him singing was "His Eye is On the Sparrow". Faith and I were known for giggling and this is one time we could not help ourselves.

****

As I sit at the dining room table thinking about the past and Hopewell Methodist Church, I can remember a lot of things. One, we had our Sunday School "room" in the back of the church with only a screen to separate us from the main part of the church. When I was very small, Grandma Vinson was our teacher. I don't remember which preacher, but one Sunday during the summer, (I was between 5 and 8 years old), we had a preacher preaching hard about going to hell and I got so scared Daddy had to go out with me. We sat in the car under the trees on the left side of the church. Sometimes Daddy would park under those trees in the summer.

I remember Marie, Mabel, and Jeannette Hinson coming to church. They were first cousins to each other. I thought they were the prettiest girls and I wanted to grow up to be just like them. I remember the wonderful hot and spicy baked beans that Cousin Gemmie Meadows used to bring to the church dinners. After Annette started playing the piano, she put some pep in our music. I was the song leader for part of this time.

One year Aunt Ethel was our Bible School teacher and she (maybe Uncle Jesse) carved a little house with steps going up to the roof out of soap. Another time, our preacher asked us all to pray for someone. This was after I was married. Aunt Ethel had not been able to come to church for a long time, so I prayed for her. Before she died she was again attending church service. I remember Mrs. Elizabeth Eckles teaching me a song, "Living for Jesus". When I joined the church and was baptized by Brother Wesley, I felt so wonderful. I also remember Brother Pittman's wife. Did you know she put on make-up during the sermon? I was a teenager then and thought she was really a very pretty lady. She also played the piano very well.

A lot of times coming home from church at night, Daddy would lead all of us in singing hymns. When I was a teenager, we had a good group of youth and I always enjoyed going to church and being with them. I remember Aunt Estelle being a leader and all the MYF socials we had. I just wish every person could have had the fellowship and closeness I felt and loved while growing up in a church like ours and a Christian home. There will always be some happy memories and some sad ones at Hopewell.

Pauline Vinson Hobbs

*(Note from AAE: I remember riding **to** church
with that family and all of us singing.)*

****

Memories of Willagene Hanners Hodge

June, 1996

Hopewell Methodist church is the first church that I remember attending. We did not live in the community and transportation was a problem, but

I have some fond memories. I remember the "all day" meetings with a big dinner spread. Living in the country and not having "light bread" often, I liked the sandwiches best. I would pass by all of the fried chicken, those big bowls of vegetables and salads for the pineapple sandwich—and then I would look for a chocolate cake.

In the cemetery, so very many of my relatives are buried—my mother and father, Lee and Gladys Hanners, my maternal grandparents, Eugene and Willa Story Riddle, my great-grandparents, Judge Aaron and Laura Jones Story and many uncles, aunts and others. One of my dearest friends, Evanelle Story Porch, who was also my cousin, is one who was buried there in more recent years.

I remember dear Aunt Ollie Vinson who taught children's Sunday School classes until near the end of her ninety six year life.

I remember the Rev. Wilbur Walton. He was the one who married Tom and me in 1941. We were married at the parsonage.

It was at Hopewell that I got my first Christian teaching. In 1948, I accepted the LORD Jesus Christ as my Savior. He is not only my Savior, but my LORD, my Helper, my Friend and much, much more. I thank God for the steadfastness of Hopewell Methodist church for over 150 years.

****

Hopewell United Methodist Church has always been a place of joy and comfort for me, but its significance in my life has changed from the time when I was a little girl. Perhaps my first memories of Hopewell are sitting on the pew during the Sunday sermon. While I enjoyed attending services with the grown-ups, I thought it was a bit long and quite often got fidgety. I remember being able to peer through the floorboard cracks and thinking that the slat pews weren't very comfortable. During the summer, I loved the cool breeze coming through the windows and listening to the birds singing or crickets chirping.

During the summer, there were fans placed on the pews so you could keep cool when there weren't any breezes blowing. The grown-ups would patiently fan themselves, and my mother would fan me to keep me cool. For some reason, I particularly remember Aunt Ollie Vinson fanning herself with a pretty fan and listening intently to the sermon.

Other memories that I cherish include warm summer nights during revivals or singings in the church. I just barely remember the beautiful old lights in the sanctuary and the moths buzzing around the light that attracted them. I particularly loved singings because I could join in singing all my favorite hymns—"Blessed Assurance", "Love, Mercy & Grace", "In the Garden", and many other beautiful songs.

Of course, my childhood memories also include Sunday School, Vacation Bible School, Easter Egg Hunts, MYF, reunions and many other church activities. The Jones/Lynch/Story Reunion in June was always fun. I loved having dinner on the ground and then playing in the grove beside the church. I always enjoyed the day right up until the grown-ups went in for the business meeting. I could not imagine what they could be talking about for so long when I was quite ready to go home and play!

Although I cherish my childhood memories, Hopewell church and community mean different things to me now. The church and people of Hopewell that I have known all my life are a joy and comfort to me. They have come to support me in times of sadness and celebrated with me during happy times.

But mostly, I am proud of how beautiful Hopewell is. It is beautiful with the love and care of its committed members and as a church that is warm and welcoming. It is a place of caring, love, kindness and inspiration—a place of beauty for the heart as well as the soul.

Faith S. Hoople

****

I remember a lot of things about Hopewell Church. Grandma Vinson was always there, or course, teaching little kids and big ones, too, about Jesus and singing songs. There were Christmas parties, Bible School, Easter egg hunts, and weddings. There were a lot of people and tears at funerals. I remember some of the older pastors, especially how their voices sounded when they preached. I remember some funny things like Grandpa Vinson sometimes went to sleep in church and snored. And, how Annette, Pauline, Barbara and I giggled every time someone smiled at us.

After I left home and was gone to Germany for a while, I remember how good it made me feel to drive up to Hopewell Church. It was a true feeling of coming home to me.

Carolyn Freeman Howard

****

OLD HOPEWELL

Reverend Wesley Otis Lynch, Jr.

Hopewell has always been a part of my memory. In a November 11, 1926, letter written by my great grandmother Nettie Jones (Artimissie Antoinette Story, sister of Judge Story and daughter of James B. Story) to my father's sister, Eva May Lynch, she writes: "Otis and family came to see us… Otis has sure got a sweet family. I don't think Otis could have done any better than when he taken Josie… Haven't they 2 sweet children. The boy is so much like your daddy" (S. H. Lynch)

I was two years old when that was written. My father made annual visits to Hopewell, visiting family and reunions. Hopewell has truly been a major part of my life.

My great great grandfather, Jeremiah Franklin Bentley, was a Methodist minister and involved in the founding of Hopewell. My great grandfather, William Herschel Lynch, served as pastor in 1875. My grandfather, Scribner Herschel Lynch (Kimmie), served as pastor in 1901. My father, Otis Lynch, and I have preached at Hopewell on many occasions.

Let me share with you some excerpts from letters written in 1894 between Lula Jones and S. H. Lynch (my grandparents). Also there are two letters from Rev. Thomas Monroe McGraw who was pastor in 1893-94. There are over thirty letters. In each one, Hopewell is spoken of in loving and exciting terms.

S. H. Lynch was in Hissop, Alabama (Coosa County) attending school. Lula (Nora Louise) Jones was the daughter of Artimissie Antoinette Story and William Carter Jones.

"February 1, 1894"

To: S. H. Lynch – from Lula Jones

"…Well Kimmie, Brother MCGraw has just come in and I will have to close and get supper…. Well it is night again. Brother McGraw did not stay with us tonight. He went to your Papa's" *(W. H. Lynch)*…. Seaborn *(Jones)* and Uncle Judge *(Story)* had their babes (Jessie Franklin Story, *(b. 10 Nov. 1893, d. 12 Dec. 1971)* and Katie Jones, *(b. 27 Sep. 1892, d. 3 Oct. 1895)* baptized last meeting."

February 4, 1894 from Hissop, Alabama

To: Miss Lula Jones from S. H. Lynch

"…I often think of that dear church and wish I could be there… But I am looking forward to some future day when we shall make old Hopewell ring with music, and have a feast from the LORD…."

May 10, 1894

To: Mr. S. H. Lynch at Hissop, Ala. From Lula Jones

"Well, Kimmie, you ought to have been with me at Hopewell last Sunday. We had the best class meeting I was ever in. We had some of the best prayers and talks at all. Oh Kimmie, how I did enjoy it. I felt like singing and shouting all the day long. Thank God oh my soul for religion, for there is no better help but God."

July 19, 1894

To: S. H. Lynch from Lula Jones

"We had a good meeting last night. Arie *(Arie Morgan Lynch, wife of James Asbury Lynch)* went home rejoicing. She came to me after the meeting and said, 'Oh, Lula, I am so happy.'"

November 23, 1894 Evergreen, Alabama

To: Sister Lula Jones from Rev. T. M. McGraw

"Bro. Gibson is on Lee *(Circuit).* He is a good man. He will do you a great deal of good. He's rough & plain, but he is good.

I preached last Sunday at a church that I organized 9 years ago *(It is on Evergreen Circuit).* The name of the church is Holly Grove. O what a happy time we all had. I thought of good old Hopewell. It has been just four weeks since I preached at Hopewell, my mind runs back away up there, and oh how sad I feel when I remember the happy times we have had at Hopewell, and not to think that these days and times are all in the past, and will never come again."

December 20, 1894

To: Lula Jones from Rev. T. M. McGraw

"…shall I ever get back to good old Hopewell anymore. I carry all to the good LORD in humble prayer."

2 May, 1895
S. H. (Kimmie) Lynch married Nora Louise (Lula) Jones
Reverend Thomas Monroe McGraw presided

I share these letters to show the events at Hopewell 102 years ago, the impact on their lives, and how they loved old Hopewell.

Hopewell had a tremendous impact on the Lynch and Jones families.

W. H. Lynch's oldest daughter, Rosalie, married Rev. Wesley Crawford Jackson.

W. H. Lynch's sons, William Arthur and Scribner Herschel became ministers.

W. A. Lynch's son, Alwyan Herschel, became a minister and missionary to Japan.

Two sons of S. H. Lynch and Lula Jones, Wesley Otis and Andrew Gladys, became ministers.

Otis' son, W. O. Jr. and Gladys' son, Jack, are ministers.

Two brothers of Lula Jones, William Seaborn and Andrew Valentine, became ministers.

Lula Jones' sister, Emma Irene, married John Leland Allen. Their son, Leon Hartwell Allen, married Estelle Vinson, a granddaughter of Judge Story.

"Old Hopewell" has served the LORD through the years. Other families could tell similar stories. We have all been blessed by Hopewell's ministry.

****

Memories taken by telephone from Mrs. Emma McConnell

I remember one minister especially, the Rev. W. C. Conner. He could sing well.

The July Revivals were always attended by large crowds from near and far.

I have pleasant memories of attending Hopewell Church. When we were having prayer meeting for a long time, I led the service several times.

Jasper, my husband, loved Hopewell Church. Before he got sick we deeded an acre of land to Hopewell Cemetery.

****

Memories of Irma McConnell By her daughter, Peggy McConnell Long

It was in the old church building. The service had not started. Bernice Vinson and I were sitting together and all of a sudden a bug started making a loud noise. Bernice got up and went out. She came back in a few minutes. The bug was making a louder noise and everybody was laughing. Bernice went out again and when she came back in, there was no more noise from that bug. She got rid of it this time.

One summer night in 1944 during church service, the preacher was talking and it was about the middle of his sermon when a group of people came in and started shouting, dancing around and singing. It broke the church service up. But Mrs. Jesse Story got up and got one of them by the collar and told them to leave and not to come back. The group left and the service continued on. This really happened. I don't know what faith they were.

****

Poem Written for Hopewell History Book
By Philip E. McVay, June 1986
Pastor of Lee Circuit 1979-1983

"The Seed of Caring"

For years you have been the "salt of the earth"
And a church shining on a hill.
And you have been devoted to the living God,
And have sought your Master's Will.
You have spread the wonderful message,
That Christians have to share.
And the greatest thing you have done for us
Is planted the seed to care.
For generations you have been a tower of strength
For a community in need.
You have been loving, kind, and thoughtful
And faithful in Word and Deed.
You've carried on the warm heart of Wesley
Into Methodism's present day.
You have been rich in tradition and creed,
But most of all you have planted a seed.
You've been a "Good Samaritan" to us
In our time of need.
You've watched us grow, and helped us
Realize the fullness of God's Dream.
You've stood by and encouraged us,
But most of all you've planted a seed.
Who are we? We are the student pastors,
And we are indebted for all your love and care.
We have gone to serve other churches…
But we take with us the precious
Seed to Care!

****

We moved into the Hopewell community when I was about ten years of age. During the depression, we had to park the car in the garage and walk to church. We were very poor and it was very hot.

I remember Mr. Doc (Vinson) and Mr. D. P. (Meadows) napping during the preaching service. It was about the only time they had time to sit down.

We had very good crowds at church. During the revivals, the church was always full.

I have so many good memories of people in the past and present.

LaVerne Clegg Miller
(died December, 1998)

****

Lucy Meadows Montague

When I grew up in Lee County, Alabama, on the south bank of Little Uchee Creek, Hopewell Church was a big part of our family life. We lived between Pleasant Grove Baptist Church and Hopewell Methodist Church. My father was a member of Pleasant Grove and mother was a devout member of Hopewell so we were always going to church, alternating between Baptist and Methodist, as neither father nor mother could/would change membership.

As I began researching my ancestry, I found that Hopewell had a big influence in my heritage. My maternal great grandparents, grandparents, and parents—Story, Browning, Meadows—were active in this church since its beginning and are buried in the adjoining cemetery. The oldest marked grave is that of James Story, my great grandfather, who was born in 1794 in North Carolina and died in 1859. I remember his grave was in an enclosed area surrounded with an iron picket fence and an elevated shingled A-line roof. Maypops, cape jasmine, and butterfly weed grew at random among the marble, granite and concrete tombstones.

One of my earliest memories of Hopewell was attending a Christmas program in the old church. Santa Claus left a little rocking chair for me under the huge cedar Christmas tree that was decorated with homemade garlands of paper and popcorn. There was no electricity for lighting then and the building was one large rectangular room with a raised pulpit across one end, heated by a wood stove in the center and flickering kerosene lamps hung on the walls to provide light for nighttime meetings.

I remember attending the funeral service for my grandmother, Frances (Fannie) Jane Browning and her brother, Judge Story, who died one day before she did. There were 2 caskets, one white for grandmother and a gray one for Uncle Judge. They were placed in front of the pulpit, parallel to each other, for the funeral service. I was about eleven years old at the time.

Revivals were held each summer at Hopewell and Pleasant Grove and the visiting preacher for each church made our home headquarters for the week. Lively discussions sometimes developed at our house when the visiting Baptist preacher challenged "Nonie" (Aunt Nora Story), who lived with us after her sister's death, with topics like "sanctification", "justification", and "falling from grace". These and other subjects were reviewed and debated each summer during revival week.

Hopewell was known for the joyful music that the congregation loved to sing. There was a foot pump organ in the early days of worship in the old church. Miss Sammie Ramsey was the first organist that I can remember. She had a special talent of coordinating hymns with sermons that made the congregation want to do their best when praising God in song. After the new sanctuary was finished, the pump organ was replaced with a piano and Miss Mildred Story was pianist for several years. When she left, Miss Adele McConnell took over the piano keyboard with much zeal and joyful spirit, sounding the notes with determination that all could hear. My sister,

Frances Meadows, substituted for Sunday School when the regular pianist was absent.

One of the most enjoyable occasions at Hopewell was the "all day singing with dinner on the grounds". Long tables were built in the shade of the trees that grew on the church property and every so often they would be covered with white tablecloths for the potluck dinner that was served at noon after a morning of singing all the old hymns of praise and worship that many could sing from memory. This noontime spread was a time for socializing as well as feasting. Everyone was ready to sample the delectable food that each family had brought for the occasion. Picnic baskets were unpacked and home cooked delicacies were spread on the table. There was always more than enough food for everyone; with platters of country ham, fried chicken, potato salad, deviled eggs, and fresh vegetable casseroles. One of my favorite desserts was lemon cheese cake that was sometimes covered with white divinity icing. Besides a big variety of cakes, there were all kinds of pies and puddings to be shared with relatives and friends. Gallons of lemonade and iced tea were soon devoured and at about 1:30 in the afternoon, a song session was called together to conclude the festivities of the day.

These are some of the memories of Hopewell that will always be with me.

****

Lauren D. Montgomery

*(Lauren Duffey M. Dempsey. Lauren married Mark
Dempsey after she wrote these memories.)*

My first memories of Hopewell start at about age five. I remember being dressed up and wearing patent leather shoes. Usually my visits to Opelika were during the summer. Years ago, before air conditioning was installed, plenty of cardboard fans were provided on all the pews. On hot summer Sundays, most of those fans were put to good use as we'd all try desperately to beat the heat.

At first, my older brother, Don, and I would attend Hopewell as the first Allen grandchildren. Later, our younger sisters, Alicia and Maria, joined us on Sundays. The Allen Family included Grandpa (Leon) Allen, Grandma (Estelle) Allen, our mother, Annette, Great Grandma (Ollie) Vinson, Uncle Hartwell, Aunt Lenora and our younger cousin, Christopher.

My earliest vivid memories of Hopewell are of Great Grandma Vinson. She was always a calming presence to us kids. She was soft spoken and could keep us amused, sometimes despite our urge to "fidget" during the Sunday Service. Grandma Vinson had a close personal relationship with God, and her sweet voice could usually be heard above most others while singing her favorite hymns. She was also a teacher. When the time came for the children to be excused for Sunday School, the youngest would eagerly scamper away to Grandma Vinson's gentle instruction.

My Grandpa Allen was a well-spoken gentleman who took the responsibilities of family and church seriously. I remember that he spoke regularly at church and was responsible for the introduction of lay speakers to the congregation. Although a quiet, dignified man of few words, he would sometimes surprise us all with his subtle sense of humor.

My Grandma Allen was, and still is, very involved in Hopewell. She shares the responsibility for maintaining the church. Hopewell is always neat, clean and comfortable. I can hardly remember a Sunday that

Grandma hasn't arrived at church long before anyone else to turn on the air conditioner or heat to prepare for Sunday services. There always seems to be a beautiful flower arrangement at the altar on Sunday. A lot of Grandma's own flowers cut from her yard have graced the sanctuary over the years. During the autumn months, Grandma Allen has still managed to dress up the church with beautifully colored fall leaves and green plants.

The time immediately following church services was no less enjoyable. I can remember countless Sunday lunches at Grandma's house. We all gathered in her dining room and shared the most delicious home-cooked meals with the preacher or someone from church who'd been asked to join us afterward. On these occasions, we could count on our cousins, Charles, Ellen and Faith Hoople, to come home with us. Faith, who is my age, was always a joy to spend time with. I feel that we grew up together although we lived so many miles apart.

During the summers, time and schedules allowing, my brother and/or sisters and I could be found at Grandma's house. Vacation Bible School and Hopewell Revivals are something we've all attended. The ladies who led our classes were very kind. One particular visit left me changed forever. At about age eight, after class, I sat on the brick steps of the church with one of our spiritual guides and accepted Christ into my life. I can think of no better place in the world for my acceptance of Him to take place!

Hopewell Methodist Church has been a source of comfort, warmth and peace for so many people. It has been a place for family and friends to gather and mourn, to rejoice, and in some cases, just catch up on each other's lives. Some of my closest relatives and family friends are buried at Hopewell. In 1985, after my grandfather died, the members of Hopewell were extremely helpful and supportive of us during our time of need.

My brother, Don, has such high regard for the institution of Hopewell that he decided to share the happiest event of his life with us by marrying his wife, Karin, at Hopewell in 1987.

We've spent many afternoons on the church lawn, catching up and enjoying the covered dishes prepared by the loving hands of some of the best cooks in the South! I'm proud to know that my family has been so involved in Hopewell Methodist church and I hope we'll be able to continue to enjoy our church this way for many years to come.

"Don's marriage to Karin did not stand the test of time. He was married a second time in the church to Ulrike Schram and they reside in Germany."

(Lauren's life ebbed away on December 7, 2010, exactly one month after her Grandmother, Estelle Vinson Allen, passed away. She is buried beside her in the Hopewell Cemetery.)

****

Yes, I have some good memories of Hopewell.

I remember when I was a girl that Brother Love was our pastor. We cleaned up the side of the church yard and the outside tables were built. Sometimes on Saturday night the girls would cook some simple food and the boys would buy it. We ate on the church steps. The money we made went to buy materials used for the building and cleaning.

On certain days in the summer, we would meet and clean the cemetery. Brother Love always had something for the teens. We would sometimes meet at different homes to talk and have chips and soft drinks.

I remember when Mrs. Meadows died suddenly at Sunday School in 1954. I was so scared. I had come to church with her and I wondered how I would get home.

Lois McConnell Moore

October 15, 1996

****

I remember the good times I had attending Sunday School in the late 1930's with Mrs. Ollie Vinson as my teacher.

I recall the construction of the fellowship hall addition around 1963. Mr. Jesse Story and other men of the church helped with the addition. Ellen and Charles Hoople led the effort to beautify and identify old grave sites in the church cemetery in the mid 1960's. About the same time, Leland Vinson, Bud Vinson, Donald Mullins, Thomas Nixon, Jesse Story, Otis Story and other helped to landscape the church's front lawn and planted the grass that is growing there today.

I have a lot of fond memories of Hopewell, especially of my three boys, Tim, Lee, and Don, attending Vacation Bible School in the mid 1960's. Some of the Bible School teachers that I recall were Ellen Hoople, Agnes Vinson, Barbara Chandler, Estelle Allen, Eula Will Mayberry, Geraldine Story, Mrs. Ollie Vinson and Lillian Paschal. All the children enjoyed the refreshment time. Providing refreshments usually were Mamie Ramsey, Louise Roberts and others.

Margie McConnell Mullins

October, 1996

(Margie died April 24, 1998.)
(I remember Margie being the most interesting
nursery S.S. teacher I ever knew.
One visual aid was churning. She actually
brought a churn and a dasher. EVA)

****

I remember so many things about Hopewell, but the most memorable events for me that happened at Hopewell were Christmas programs and my wedding.

I remember as a little girl dressing up as an angel for a Christmas play at Hopewell. I believe I was four years old. I remember wearing a white gown with wings attached and a small piece of gold garland wrapped around my head. I don't remember if I said any lines but a lot of people came to see the program.

Another year, I played Mary in a Christmas play at Hopewell. I was fifteen years old. My role was to sit at the manger scene and be Jesus' mother. Again, there were a lot of people. Afterwards, we had a reception in the fellowship hall.

My wedding was held at Hopewell. I was married on March 28, 1992, on a beautiful spring afternoon. The temperature that day was in the 70's. The sanctuary was decorated with teal bows on the altar and pews and candelabras stood behind the altar rail and were lit. My husband, Alan, wore a black tuxedo with an ivory shirt and an ivory lily boutonniere. My dress was made of ivory lace with short capped sleeves and a boat neck collar. I carried a bouquet of carnations, lilies and roses. There were about fifty people in attendance. The reception was held in the fellowship hall of the church. The hall was decorated with brightly colored balloons and beautiful green plants. Our wedding cake was decorated with pink, yellow and lavender lilies. We had punch, mints, and peanuts. Alan's Corvette was decorated with blue and yellow streamers and yellow and red balloons.

Lea Ann Chandler Nhoybouakong

****

There are so many memories of Hopewell it is hard to know where to begin. Next to home, Hopewell Church was a main part of my life all during my growing up years. One of my first memories of Hopewell is Sunday School. My mother always saw that we got up, did our chores and dressed for Sunday School on Sunday mornings. I remember learning the songs, the Bible verses and listening to the Bible stories. I went through all the classes from Beginners to Young Adult. One of my favorite classes was our Young Adult class. We had a large class of eager and interested young adults with a wonderful teacher, Mrs. Leon Allen (Aunt Estelle).

Another favorite was our night-time services. In my early years it was known as Christian Endeavor, later Methodist Youth Fellowship (MYF). I believe the work I did in these services greatly benefited me later.

The Quarterly conference still remains a fond memory. We had the conferences each quarter at a different church on the charge. We had the morning sermon, dinner on the grounds and the afternoon business session. As children, we could stay outside and play during the afternoon.

To be sure, there have been many favorite people, teachers, relatives and preachers at Hopewell. Two preachers I remember fondly were Brother Wilbur Walton and Brother Robert Wilson.

Hopewell Cemetery is one of my favorite places on earth. It is one of the most peaceful, comforting places I know. "Precious Memories, How They Linger."

Marie Hinson Nixon

(Cemeteries are sacred to me, too. I wonder about
those who have died and are buried there.
What struggles did they have? How did they seek God?
Their stories are probably similar to ours.
We are all held in the "Hand of the LORD".)EVA

****

Hopewell United Methodist church, known as Hopewell Methodist Protestant Church when I was a child, has been dear to my family as long as I can remember. I suppose I can say we were active members. At least our parents, John Franklin and Mary Belle Allen Lynch, were. Papa must have been church clerk. He sat at a table up front at our annual conference, and other times too, to read minutes and record actions being taken. I believe this annual conference was the third Saturday either in May or June and everybody carried a basket lunch and spread it on long table on the lawn. If I remember correctly, everybody hoped to have fresh green beans and potatoes by this time. Of course, there were a lot of other good dishes too, like fried chicken and blackberry pie.

During the conference and at worship services, Mama, my sisters, Libby and Mary, and I sat near the front on a bench made of rough lumber with wide spaces between. They were not called pews then. We hardly dared raise an eyebrow, wiggle around, giggle or cause any disturbance.

Protracted meetings in the summer, after lay-by-time, were the highlight of the year. Even after we moved to town, that is Opelika, Mama and we girls would go back to attend. We would alternate staying with our church friends at night and were included with others for noon dinner. Church members always prepared a "Sunday go to meeting" dinner and expected the pastor, visiting preacher and others to go home with them for a noon meal.

Before we moved, Libby, our niece, Ima Riddle, and I made a profession of faith and were baptized on the same Sunday. I'm sure we were too young to fully realize what this meant but we had talked it over among ourselves and then with our parents… We didn't get to attend as regularly after we moved, but, with Christian home training, our faith grew and prepared us for active responsibility and service in our respective churches.

After our parents died, Mama on November 21, 1929, and Papa on March 16, 1940, we seldom attended at Hopewell. Libby and I have had the joy of attending family reunions in the church and have been delighted to see the growth and the recent building expansion.

I treasure the memory of the fellowship we had with families who were there then and those still there, and lovingly remember those who had a part in our lives.

Lola Lynch Orr
((Lola died October 6, 1997)

****

Earnest (Sonny) Paschal, Jr.

Probably my nicest memories are when I was a small boy five or six years old being in Grandma Vinson's Kindergarten Sunday School Class. She was a very interesting teacher, showing us Bible pictures and telling the meaning of them. We learned Bible verses and sang many songs.

I might not have been that attentive at Worship Service. I remember looking out the window and seeing the bees flying around outside.

Sometimes some of the older people would go to sleep. One time our preacher (I don't remember which one) hit the top of the pulpit very loudly with a book, I guess to awaken the sleeping!

As a child, I watched the ushers taking up the offering and wondered where all that money went. Now, I realize it is needed for many causes to support the church. Also, I watched a few people put a bill in the plate and then take some money out. I wondered about that.

The most frightening thing happened when I was about twelve years old. My Sunday School class was held in the corner where the choir is now. I think two other classes were held in the sanctuary. Mrs. D. P. Meadows (Cousin Gemmie) taught what I called the old folks class. She was a very interesting teacher and I often watched her instead of listening to my teacher. (I don't remember who my teacher was at the time.) Anyway one Sunday morning as she stood teaching she fell backwards, then down on her knees. She had died of a sudden heart attack. That was my first experience of witnessing death. I remember several nights after that I dreamed about this shocking incident.

I joined the church at Hopewell in 1954 when the Rev. Glen Sirmon was pastor.

****

Millie Sims Peters

My mother, Mildred Elizabeth Jones Sims, was born and grew up in the area near Hopewell Methodist Church. I am not sure whether she was ever a member there but know that many family members on her father's side are buried in the Hopewell Cemetery. Mother was born January 6, 1901, to Emily Hester Cadenhead Jones and William Seaborn Jones. She was the third of four daughters born to this couple. Her oldest sister died at age 2 of whooping cough before the second child was born so the family consisted of three girls. That first daughter is buried at Hopewell. Mother always referred to her as her "baby sister" since she never grew up. I believe that many of mother's childhood playmates were relatives who lived nearby. Her family connections were complicated to describe as her father's widowed uncle (by marriage) married an old maid sister of her mother." The widowed uncle had children and he and his second wife had other children, all of whom lived nearby and I assume were possible playmates of hers. She was especially fond of the Lynch brothers (Gladys and W. O.) who later became Methodist ministers. She told of having Gladys as a young man practice his sermons for her while standing on a tree stump in the yard. I believe they were first cousins. William Seaborn Jones, her father, was also a Methodist minister in the old Methodist Protestant faith and the family moved often. He always served more than one church and she often spoke of traveling with him to preach—driving the buggy while he practiced his sermon. She, therefore, did not spend all of the early years in Lee County, but she remembered them fondly and always looked forward to the Hopewell reunions. I think that was because the attendees would include people with whom she shared memories of childhood and memories of loved ones who were no longer alive. Mother was 43 years old when I was born and I never knew many of the people she remembered. Naturally as a child I didn't always listen carefully to her

---

" (The widowed uncle was my maternal grandfather, Judge Aaron Story.
He married Sultana Elizabeth Cadenhead in 1892.)EVA

reminiscing. She of course repeated them and I am certain that she had a special love for the times she could return to Hopewell. As long as she was able she attended the Hopewell reunions in June. We continued to bring her when possible after we moved to Tennessee. Mother lived to be 94 and died May 27, 1995. Unfortunately in her last years she suffered from senile dementia and all memories of people and places were gone. I learned in caring for her in those last years that this type disease robs you of your loved ones before they are actually gone from this earth because the shared memories of your past together are gone and therefore your relationship endures a radical change. You still have a loved one, but you can no longer say, "Do you remember when…" and expect a response.

****

Submitted by John and Susan Scott Porch

January, 1997

Even though I did not "grow up" in Hopewell, there are a lot of things that I remember about the church from visiting Granddaddy and Grandmom Story. I remember Mrs. Dorsey playing the piano and Mr. Burns leading the singing. After church, Mr. Burns used to come over to Granddaddy's house and we'd all sit in the living room while my sister Carol played and Mr. Burns sang some more. We used to come up for Bible School in the summer, and there was always a good reason to have a dinner out on the picnic tables.

From the time we moved to Lee County and I began attending Hopewell regularly, the memories are more complete. I remember the way the church welcomed new pastors with a pounding, and how the people always were supportive of the pastor, working out their differences in a peaceful, Christian way. There were also many Lay Speakers that came and spoke to us, like Ken Marsh, Ken McKemie, Hoyt Roberts, and Dick Lane. We gave them an appreciation supper one night, and they were quite touched by the church's thanks. There were several things added to help the building itself, like the brick walkway, the steeple, the stained glass windows and a microphone and speakers.

I met Susan in December of 1983, the first Sunday she walked in the sanctuary. I'm especially glad that three years later we were married in that same room.

There were several times that I would go over to the church late at night and pray. It was always easy to feel the LORD's presence when everything was so quiet.

John Porch

****

My memories of Hopewell only go back a few years, but even in a short time, the church had a great impact on my life. We were married at Hopewell in 1986, and for several years after that, we lived across the street from the church. Many peaceful nights were spent on our front porch, talking with God while watching the light shine forth from the steeple window at the church. That church on the hill became a landmark for our early family memories, and we want our children to grow up knowing its history.

Susan Porch

****

Bobbie Hightower Pate

9/12/1997

Hopewell Church has always been a happy and comfortable place for me. It was safe and well cared for. We all knew each other and cared for one another.

The white folks and the colored folks got along well. There was no stealing or bad behavior. I wish the whole world could be like the Hopewell Church area was when I lived there. Maybe we had a taste of Heaven right here on earth.

****

Overene Jones Risher

Daughter of Jewel Lynch Jones Brice
August 5, 1997

Mama's great grandfather, Jerry (T or F) Bentley, born in Georgia (1818) was one of the founders of Hopewell. His daughter, Jemima Frances Bentley, married William Hershell Lynch in 1861, so that's how the Lynch name got started in our family.

I have no record of when any of Mama's siblings joined the church, but her father, Rev. Arthur Lynch, served Lee Circuit in 1924 and 1925, so some of them probably did join at Hopewell. *(note from aae: I found several of them in a 1924 roster of members.)*

Mama's sister, Zada Lynch Johnson was 93 in June of this year (1997). Her half- sister, Joyce Lynch Todd is in Dallas, Texas. She was in the third set of children and is younger than I am.

As for memories of what Mama said about Hopewell—She loved the reunions because they brought back memories of her youth and she always pointed out the spot where her grandfather's house was and told us he had a little store in the edge of the yard. She loved talking about that little store. We all loved going out into the cemetery and finding all the old graves.

Since Mama died in 1993, I think that puts 1992 as the last time we were at Hopewell.

I had forgotten that Mama's sister, Nellie Lynch Betts, had moved back to Opelika about the time our family moved to Rock Hill. Her daughter, Betty Conner Betts, came to visit recently. She lives near Jackson, Mississippi.

Note: Overene Jones Risher also included a list of circuits and churches served by Rev. William Arthur Lynch taken from a hand-written page in a Bible. This information is included in the Jones/Lynch/Story Reunion section in a 2004 report given by W. O. Lynch, Jr.)

****

Linda Clegg Smallwood

9-29-97

My first vivid recollection of Hopewell is as a small child attending worship services every Sunday morning. I also remember Bible School, egg hunts, revivals, Christmas programs, specials on Mother's Day and Father's Day and very early sunrise services at Easter, and especially MYF.

I have very fond memories of "going with" my parents, Walter and Jewel Clegg, seeing my Grandmother, Mrs. Glennie Herring, and other members of the Church such as: Mrs. Ollie Vinson, Mr. and Mrs. Jesse Story, Mr. and Mrs. Otis Story, Mr. and Mrs. Geoffrey Story, Mrs. Bernice Freeman, Mr. and Mrs. Luther Hinson, Mr. and Mrs. Leon Allen, Mr. and Mrs. Charles Hoople, Mr. and Mrs. Grady Chadwick, Mr. and Mrs. Buster Brown, Mr. and Mrs. Earnest Paschal, Mr. and Mrs. Wayne Freeman, Mr. and Mrs. Ralph Bell, Mr. and Mrs. Thomas Nixon and others. I cherish my youth memories of Marietta, Kenneth and Benny Story, Annette, Hartwell and Lenora Allen, Jasper Brown, Freida, Mickie and Diane Foster, Sheryl Nixon, and Sonny and Terry Paschal and others.

I shall always remember Rev. & Mrs. Charles Pittman, Rev. & Mrs. Sam Lowery, Rev. and Mrs. Bobby Holliday, Rev. and Mrs. Dick Cobb, Rev. and Mrs. Andy Knight and Rev. and Mrs. Randall.

I was married to William Gerald (Jerry) Smallwood in this church in July, 1966, with the Revs. Dick Cobb and Sam Lowery officiating. Our three children (Kim, Kristi, and Keith) were christened here in 1968, 1970 and 1974.

My saddest memories are the funerals of family and loved ones I've attended. My grandparents, (L. R. and Rebecca Clegg and Floyd and Glennie Herring), my father (Walter Clegg) and my uncles (Martin and Herman Herring) are buried there.

I remember my parents working in many areas of the church...UMW meetings, cutting grass, cleaning the church, upkeep of the cemetery, being Sunday School officers and on the Board of Trustees.

Hopewell is situated in one of the loveliest locations in Lee County... whether at sunrise or sunset, the view is breathtaking!

This church and many of the church families will always have a special place in my heart.

(Since she wrote this, her mother has also been buried in the Hopewell Cemetery.)

****

Alicia Childress Spado

November 15, 1997

Since I never lived in Opelika, Alabama, just visited my family there, most of my memories of Hopewell Methodist Church are simple ones. I remember going to Sunday School class. Both of my Grandmothers used to teach Sunday School: Grandma Vinson taught the little children and Grandma Allen taught the teens, and later an adult class. My family was very active in the church. I remember Grandma Allen being treasurer and

Grandpa Allen being a part of the offering time during church. He was also Sunday School Superintendent. My sister, Maria, and I always loved to put a shiny quarter or a dollar in the offering plate as it went by. I also remember listening to my mother, Annette, play the piano a few times. I always loved when it was time to sing at church. My favorite song when I was young was "Standing on the Promises"! I guess that was because I could sing at the top of my lungs and no one cared.

The most fun times I can remember at Hopewell were the reunions. Grandma Allen would always fix food and after church we would all go outside to eat. Everyone always filled up those long white tables with good food. One of the most memorable of those would have to be June, 1986, the year my family dressed up in 1800's outfits, celebrating the 140th year of the church. My mother, sister, and I had on those long dresses and my brother had his top hat complete with cane. If I recall it was very hot that summer and of course the dresses probably made it feel worse.

(All dressed up for the 140th anniversary celebration of Hopewell)

There were special occasions that my family shared at the church. I remember my grandparent's 50th wedding anniversary. I was always so amazed how many people my grandparents knew and how much everyone loved them. I still am. I got to sing at their anniversary celebration. I don't remember how good it was, but I was pleased to be a part of their special day. My brother, Donnie, got married at Hopewell. I remember spending hours decorating for the event. It was soon after Christmas and the church was filled with poinsettias.

Unfortunately there were also sad memories at Hopewell. I remember my Grandmother Vinson's funeral and my Grandfather Allen's funeral being held there with their burials being in the church cemetery. There were so many flowers and friends at both funerals. It was very touching to see how many people cared about both of them. Since I am grown and don't get to spend as much time in Alabama as I did as a child, I always look forward to going to church when I am there. My daughter, Alexis, has also attended and I hope she will always enjoy going. Hopewell has brought me a lot of good memories. I hope it will do the same for her and for my son, Mikey. I think my daughter's favorite part, besides the singing, is when the preacher calls all the children up to the front and tells them about the message in a way that they can understand. I think it's great. I guess the best thing about Hopewell throughout the years has always been the people. They have always been good to my family and I know that no matter where I go I will always feel at home when I come back to Hopewell.

(Note from editor: Since she wrote this, Alicia has lived in Lee County on the farm that belonged to her maternal grandparents for a number of years and has been an active member of Hopewell Church.)

****

I remember going to Hopewell Church when we were at Grandmother's in the summer in Grandpapa Jones' wagon. This is all I remember about going to church except the services were long. My mother and papa died in their 40's. They are buried in Hopewell Cemetery. Later, I have been to some Jones, Lynch, Story Reunions.

Thelma Lynch Williams

Daughter of Rev. Kim and Lula Jones Lynch
Died August 1, 1997 in Parkerville, West Virginia

****

(Oldest church image)

I am unsure of the year of this photo, but it had to be after 1925, when this building was erected, and before 1941. The Sunday School rooms were built to the left of the sanctuary when facing the church in 1951-52. I like to think the two figures our front might have been my grandmother on the right (Laura Olivia Story Vinson, 1884-1980) and her step mother on the left (Sultana Elizabeth Cadenhead Story, 1857-1953). *(I have a photo of my brother and me on the steps, probably made in 1940. There was no tree then, but I seem to remember shrubs around the porch, so my guess is this was made in the 1930's. Annette A Edwards)*

Hopewell Cemetery

Then and Now

On a peaceful, windswept hill behind the Hopewell United Methodist Church rest early residents of the Hopewell Community along with many more recent church members, community residents, family members of those interred, and others. The actual beginning date of the cemetery is not known. The earliest marked gravesite is that of James Story, who died January 4, 1859. Because the church was on this property several years prior to that *(History of Hopewell Methodist Protestant Church 1846 – 1896 by Estelle Allen Vinson),* it well may be that undated, and possibly, unmarked graves precede 1859. The second oldest marked grave is that of Sarah Jane Browning, wife of James Browning on whose property the Church was built. *(History by E.V.A. and* www.glorecords.blm.gov). She died on March 7, 1862. An unmarked slab near her grave is believed to be that of James Browning, who also died circa 1862. *(http://files.usgwarchives.net/al/russell/court/probate/ebrowning.txt)* Other early graves include those of members of the Jones, Deas, Johnson, Blalock, and Browning families –early settlers of the Hopewell Community. A grave marker for Isaac Dozier (or possibly Rozier), death date February 19, 1879, has been found in a second area of the cemetery. There are additional sunken areas that appear to be unmarked graves. This area, previous grown up in trees and underbrush, was re-discovered in recent years when the brushy growth and some trees were cleared away. Several community members remember that there was said to be a cemetery there, and some of the oldest church members and friends, when questioned, even remembered having seen small markers. Unfortunately, anyone who could tell the history of that area of the cemetery is no longer living. It is believed that these graves might be those of workers for early Hopewell settlers and of those workers families. This area is now incorporated as part of the Hopewell Cemetery and will be designated with a marker.

Before the Hopewell Church and Cemetery property was deeded to the Church, it was first owned by the Browning family – James, and later his descendants. In 1880 Judge Aaron Story purchased this property. He and his wife, Sultana Elizabeth Story, deeded the property to Hopewell in 1900 *(Lee County, Alabama, Courthouse, Deed Book Reference 52, pages 298-299)*. In 1965, additional property was deeded to the Church for the purpose of enlarging the cemetery by Jasper McConnell *(Hopewell Methodist Church Official Board Minutes, April and June, 1965)*. The Church continued ownership of the Cemetery until December, 2009, when the Hopewell Cemetery Association was formed and the Church deeded the Cemetery property to the Association. The Association is a 501(c)(3) non-profit corporation. Its purposes, as listed in the Articles of Incorporation are "to provide a place for burial where perpetual care and attendance may be given and where respect and devotion may be given and tendered towards those who are placed therein, to provide for a trust fund in order to fulfill the above purpose to maintain and care for the cemetery and for other and necessary items in order to fulfill the above stated purposes."

Notations in church records for the years 1961 – 2004 illustrate the concern and care that church members gave to the cemetery. Many instances of cemetery cleaning and maintenance are mentioned, and on several occasions equipment was purchased and/or repaired for the purpose of maintaining the cemetery. The balances in the cemetery fund fluctuated with donations ("generous donations" at times) and with expenditures over the years. Various church members chaired or were part of the Cemetery Committee through the years. Mr. Otis Story was a long-time chairman of the Cemetery Committee, and the cemetery was dear to his heart. Other Chairmen include Mr. Walter Clegg and Mr. Jasper Brown. The trustees of the Church were also an important part of cemetery planning and expenditures.

In August, 1965, "Mrs. [Ellen] Hoople volunteered to chair a committee to identify and mark the 280 'unknown' graves in the cemetery. Mrs. [Estelle] Allen moved that an Identification and Grave Marker Committee be established and a separate fund so designated; Mrs. G. L. Story seconded; motion carried. Mrs. Hoople stated committee members were Mrs. M.N. Vinson, Mr. Otis Story, Mr. Herron McConnell, and Mr. Jesse Story." *(Hopewell Methodist Church Official Board Minutes, August, 1965)* In September, 1966, Mrs. Hoople reported that after one year of the Grave Marker Project's existence, the Committee had placed 37 markers for graves that had been identified with names and 58 plain, blank markers. There is not another report recorded until May, 1969, when Mr. Otis Story noted that 10 markers had recently been ordered and funds were needed for about 20 more to complete the project. In December, 1969, the Grave Marker Fund was nearly ready to be reported out. A number of the "unknown" graves were identified and marked, some with names when that could be determined and some with the plain, blank markers. At present there are 251 plain markers without names. Some of these are smaller than those added during the marking project and some are older, unmarked stones. Many, though, are of the style of those added during the project.

In February, 1989, Church records indicate that work was progressing on the cross project, a memorial to Mrs. Evanelle Porch (daughter of Otis Story) who had passed away on January 12, 1988. The cross project was completed in March and was dedicated at the Easter Sunrise Service that year.

Several enumerations of the graves in the Hopewell Cemetery have been done. One was done in 1952, and updated in 1966 in connection with the grave marker project. A committee from the Genealogical Society of East Alabama compiled an enumeration which was published in its journal Tap Roots *(Vol. 10, No. 4, April 1973)*. In 2011 Linda and Ben Story, aided by other family members, updated records, added family relationships and printed a new listing. This listing was further updated and revised by Ken and Carol Story for Hopewell UMC's 170th Anniversary celebration in 2016.

At present the Hopewell Cemetery has 675 known graves. The orientation of the graves is basically east-west, though the graves are certainly not all in straight rows. One might speculate that the orientation varies as it does because of the location of the sun in the sky at the time a grave was dug. There is more variability in the positioning of the older graves than in those from more recent years. Of the 675 graves, 423 are identified and marked with stones bearing the names of the interred, 252 have been identified as graves and have uninscribed stones. There are at least six sunken areas that appear to be possible grave sites. In the second area of the cemetery, only Isaac Dozier's grave has been identified. His marker is broken; plans are to provide a new marker for that grave and, additionally, to mark the areas that appear to be graves.

Hopewell Cemetery, like many older cemeteries, has quite a variety of grave marker types. There are twenty-seven plots, some older – some newer- that have curbing or coping; the materials used to construct these vary from concrete, to concrete blocks, to more polished stone. Ledger stones cover over 125 of the graves. Ledger stones are large (usually about 3'x 6' but some smaller for children's graves) rectangular grave markers laid flat over a grave or set on top of box tombs. Often the ledger is inscribed with information about the deceased. Some of these are white marble, some granite; others appear to have been made of cement. Fifty-three of the graves are of the box tomb type. These resemble a rectangular box with a flat top to hold a ledger stone and were popular in Alabama during the first half of the nineteenth century. Several of both the ledger and the box tomb type have extensions of cement-type material, lower than the ledger or tomb at the foot of the grave, giving sort of an "apron" effect.

Over 175 graves at Hopewell are marked with headstones: upright markers with a base. Most are inscribed with information about the deceased, some have epitaphs, and many have decorative carvings. Some 15% of these also have footstones. Some of the footstones designate military affiliation. One interesting footstone is actually a bench which gives a cemetery visitor a place for resting and contemplation. A tablet stone set vertically into the ground and having no base marks over 20 of Hopewell's graves. Many of these indicate military service.

Well over half of the graves have flat, rectangular markers set flush with the ground. Most of these are the markers that were placed during the Marker Project in the mid- and late-1960s. Other types of markers found in the cemetery are three obelisks (four-sided tapered shafts of stone), a chimney-shaped marker, and two small metal crosses. Statuary, including lambs, angels, and baby shoes are found on some headstones.

Grave marker designs at Hopewell Cemetery are quite interesting. Traditional designs etched into the stones include bells, angels, Bibles, doves, crosses, praying hands, flower motifs (by far the most popular design), fruit, kneeling children, hearts, lamps, scrolls, entwined wedding rings, baby shoes, and hands pointing upward. There are also designs indicating occupations and hobbies: a United Methodist Clergy design, an airplane, heavy earth-moving equipment, a mortar and pestle, flying ducks, fish, and bird dogs. Of course, there are the inscriptions and designs indicating military service. Most of these also indicate in which war the interred served.

Those buried in Hopewell Cemetery represent Confederate States of America veterans who served in the Civil War, World War I veterans, World War II veterans (one a Spar in the U.S. Coast Guard), Korean Conflict veterans, and Viet Nam veterans. Some inscriptions indicate the branch of service: U.S. Army, U.S. Navy, and U.S. Coast Guard. Hopewell Cemetery soldiers serving the Confederate States of America include early settlers in the community and several sets of relatives. Those whose graves are marked as Confederate veterans are:

William D. Cooley – Co B 13 AL Inf
Hugh P. Johnson – AL Home Guard
Martin K. Johnson – Co B 47 AL Inf
W. A. Lamb - Co F6 AL Inf

Marcellus Martin – Co K 34 AL Inf
William F. McConnell – Co K 34 AL Inf
Hiram Riddle – Co F 45 AL Inf ***
Jesse Riddle - Co F AL Inf
Daniel Brooks Story – Co K 34 AL Inf
Martin B. Williams – Co E 39 AL Inf

A listing done by Edna Ward of Opelika including not only those whose markers are at Hopewell but also those whose obituaries and other records indicate military service names B. A. U. McConnell (Co K 34 AL Rgt), Ezra Butler (Dawson's Artillery), and Robert Isaac Jones and William Carter Jones (both of Co A Jacque's Btn Columbus Guards). We assume these are all Civil War Veterans.

World War I veterans interred in the Hopewell Cemetery include Jesse Eugene Horne (Pvt Co 360 Engrs), Allen Johnson (Pvt Med Dept), Zeke H. Jones (Pvt US Army), and William J. Royal (Pvt 328 Inf). These are the soldiers who have markers; of course, there may be others that are not designated.

Those marked as veterans of World War II are Alma Ruth Roberts Barker (Spar S1 US Coast Guard), John Hansel Brown (Cpl US Army Air Corps), Carl J. Burdell, Sr (S Sgt US Army), Frederick Harold Foster (World War II), Robert G. Holman (S2 US Navy), Carl H. Lynch (PFC US Army), and Willie Ralph Sanders (Lt. US Navy). Since this was first written, Earnest C. Paschal, Sr. (1922-2016) has passed. He was a WWII Army veteran (1st Calv Div, 7th Reg, Troup E) in the Pacific Theater.

*** The "Census of Enumeration of Confederate Soldiers Residing in Alabama, 1907," found in Vol. 32, No. 4 (April 1995) Tap Roots published by the Genealogical Society of East Alabama, contains information regarding Hiram Riddle. He began his service in Co F, 45 AL Infantry, but three months later was transferred to Co B, 45th AL, where he had a brother also in Co B. However, the only brother whose military records have been located so far have all been in Co F, 45th AL Inf. Hiram did have three younger brothers who possibly were in the Confederate Army. No records have been found for them. The writing for Hiram's younger brother on the census record for 1850 is difficult to read, but it appears to be Jesse. So, the Jesse listed above may, indeed, be Hiram's brother as well.

As noted on their markers, James Berry, Jr. served as PFC, US Army in Korea, Ralph Hall, Jr. served as a Sgt, US Army in Viet Nam, Earnest Clifton Paschal, Jr. served as a Sp4, US Army in Viet Nam, and James A. Hobbs, Jr. served in both Korea and Viet Nam (S Sgt, US Army).

There are a number of other veterans, as noted on their markers, who served in the military. The war in which they served may have been left off the marker or, perhaps, they served their country during peacetime. These are US Army veterans Martin Herring, James Donald Mullins, and Owen Horace Story. US Navy veteran is Daniel Bobby Story, an AT 3, and US Marine veteran is Lydle Cosby Dunson.

The timelines of these veterans parallel the history of the Hopewell Cemetery and community – from the mid-1800s to the present. An additional part of this history is shown by the surnames found on the tombstones that also are found on original land grants made in the late 1830s – 1860: Bentley, Blalock, Browning, Eckles, Hunt, Lynch, McConnell, Royals, Story. *(U.S. Bureau of Land Management: General Land Office Records)*. In fact, the land on which the cemetery exists is part of a land grant received by James Browning on March 15, 1851 – a land grant signed by President Millard Fillmore. (See copy of land grant at end of this section.)

One of the early citizens of the Hopewell community was Hugh P. Johnson. Mr. Johnson served as a Justice of the Peace *(Tap Roots, Vol. 45, No. 1, July 2007)*. He also had a business, and his journal/account book contains the names of numerous people who did business with him, lived in the Hopewell area, and are buried in Hopewell Cemetery. Appearing in the journal is the Bentley family name. Jemima Bentley married Rev. W. H. Lynch and both are buried at Hopewell. W.H. is named in the journal in years from 1866 – 1882. Also having transactions listed are Blalocks, Chadwicks, Echoles (Eckles), Hunt, Jones (Clayton Jones is among the earlier names in the cemetery and many of his descendants are buried there as well). Robert and William Jones are also listed and are buried at Hopewell. Newton Martin and other Martins are named. William McConnell, who had one of the early land grants, also did business with Mr. Johnson as did other McConnells. Other names found in Mr. Johnson's journal and on the Hopewell Cemetery list are James A. G. Ramsey and other Ramseys, Hiram Riddle, Jesse Riddle, Judge Aaron Story, James Story and his wife, Ellen Duke, and Daniel Brooks Story. *(Tap Roots, Vol. 26, No. 2, Oct. 1988)* Mr. Johnson, like many of the men and women from the early days of the Hopewell Community, has numbers of descendants buried in the Hopewell Cemetery, some who died as recently as 2016. The lives of many of these families were entwined as members of one family married members of other families in the community. A fascinating history of the area can be found among the tombstones in this peaceful, country cemetery.

(Note that a list of those buried in Hopewell Cemetery with markers can be found at FindAGrave.com) (An interment listing by location can be had for $10.00 by contacting Carol and Ken Story, 5250 Le e Rd. 175, Salem AL 36874 or by email contact at csmstory@yahoo.com.

THE UNITED STATES OF AMERICA,

CERTIFICATE
No. *18,543.*

To all to whom these Presents shall come, Greeting:

WHEREAS *James Browning, of Russell County Alabama*

has deposited in the GENERAL LAND OFFICE of the United States, a Certificate of the REGISTER OF THE LAND OFFICE at *Montgomery* whereby it appears that full payment has been made by the said

James Browning. according to the provisions of the

Act of Congress of the 24th of April, 1820, entitled "An act making further provision for the sale of the Public Lands," for

the North East quarter of the North East quarter of Section twenty Six, in Township eighteen, of Range twenty seven East, in the District of Lands subject to Sale at Montgomery, Alabama, Containing forty acres, and Seven and a half hundredths of an Acre:

according to the official plat of the survey of the said Lands, returned to the General Land Office by the SURVEYOR GENERAL, which said tract has been purchased by the said *James Browning,*

NOW KNOW YE, That the **United States of America,** in consideration of the Premises, and in conformity with the several acts of Congress, in such case made and provided, HAVE GIVEN AND GRANTED, and by these presents DO GIVE AND GRANT, unto the said *James Browning,*

and to *his* heirs, the said tract above described: TO HAVE AND TO HOLD the same, together with all the rights, privileges, immunities, and appurtenances of whatsoever nature, thereunto belonging, unto the said *James Browning*

and to *his* heirs and assigns forever.

In Testimony Whereof, I, *Millard Fillmore* PRESIDENT OF THE UNITED STATES OF AMERICA, have caused these Letters to be made PATENT, and the SEAL of the GENERAL LAND OFFICE to be hereunto affixed.

Given under my hand, at the CITY OF WASHINGTON, the *fifteenth* day of *March* in the Year of our Lord one thousand eight hundred and *fifty one* and of the Independence of the United States the Seventy *fifth*

BY THE PRESIDENT: *Millard Fillmore*

By *Alex. McCormick aspt.* Sec'y.

E. S. Terry RECORDER of the General Land Office.

JONES-LYNCH-STORY Families and Reunions

by Annette Allen Edwards
(taken from a variety of sources)

The Jones, Lynch and Story families were a significant part of the history of Hopewell United Methodist Church.

I do know that there were some early reunions of these families that were not held at the church and there is at least one picture of one of these gatherings.

Early Jones Lynch Story reunion

(This must have been in 1949 judging from my sister's size. My father is holding her in front right of picture.)

However, we have records of attendees meeting at the church on June 28, 1981, June 27, 1982, June 26, 1983, and June 24, 1985. My mother made a note in this record book that she did not have an attendance record for 1986, but that it was large. It probably coincided with the Church Anniversary celebration. Other gatherings of this group took place in 1990, June 23, 1991, 1995, and again at 150th Church Anniversary in 1996. Mainly due to the efforts of W. O. Lynch, Jr. and my mother, Estelle Vinson Allen, the group began to meet again annually on June 25, 2000. They met on August 4, 2001, July 20, 2002, July 19, 2003, July 17, 2004, July 16, 2005, and July 15, 2006. W. O. died after the 2005 meeting. At the 2006 meeting, it was decided to meet every 2 years. We met on July 19, 2008, July 17, 2010, and July 21, 2012. Interest dwindled and no further gatherings have occurred.

The following is a synopsis of Jones/Lynch/Story interrelationships and their connections to Hopewell church which I presented to the reunion gathering in 2005:

SOME JONES LYNCH STORY/HOPEWELL CHURCH CONNECTIONS

1846 – Hopewell Church first recorded in Ala. Methodist Protestant Church

1850 – According to 1850 Census, land where church stands was owned by plantation owner, Thomas Browning, who later sold it to Judge Aaron Story. It was on Mt. Jefferson Circuit then.

1852 – Russell Circuit started

1875 – W. H. Lynch, pastor

1876 – Lee Circuit started

1890-1910 – J. A. Story, lay pastor at Goat Rock Church

April, 1900 – J. A. Story & Sultana Story deeded land to Church

1901 – Scribner Herschel (Kim) Lynch, pastor (W. O.'s grandfather)

1917 or 1918 – Kim Lynch held revival (Mama joined church)

1924-1925 – Wm. Arthur Lynch, pastor (licensed in 1901)

1925 - New church (present sanctuary) built

Pastors to go out from Hopewell:
Rev. Bentley
Rev. Cooper Martin (grandson of James Story)
Rev. Seaborn Jones (son of William Carter Jones)
Rev. Andrew Jones (son of William Carter Jones)
Rev. Wesley Otis Lynch, Sr. (son of Kim Lynch)
Rev. Andrew Gladys Lynch (son of Kim Lynch)
Rev. Alwyan Herschel Lynch (son of William Arthur Lynch)
Rev. Jack Lynch (son of Andrew Gladys Lynch)
Rev. G. L. Story, Jr. (son of Geoffrey Lee Story, Sr. (great, great, great grandson of William Story, Sr.)
Also Daniel Frank Story (Exhorter) 1870-1885

(The following family names and groupings is very exclusive. It basically is to show inter-family marriages...)

JONES

William Clayton Jones b. 1812 in GA, d. 1874 Hopewell community, Lee Cty, AL

m. 1837 Monroe, GA to Rebecca Lassiter b. 1818, GA, d. 1911, Salem AL

<u>10 children</u>

1) **Elizabeth**
2) Mary
3) **Martha**
4) Robert
5) **William Carter**
6) **John**
7) **Rebecca**
8) L. O.
9) T. C.
10) G. A.

XX 1) Elizabeth -1838-1905 m. Daniel Brooks Story in 1857

XX 3) Martha m. Alva Silas Story

Sisters married brothers (sons of William Story, Jr.). Their brother, **John (6)** married Daniel Brooks and Alva's sister. Hydricks & Edwards come from union of Martha/Alva.

XX 5) William Carter 1845-1919 m. Artimissi Antinette Story in 1869

Brother married Story, first cousin of brothers that married his sisters. Artimissi was daughter of James B. Story and 3rd wife Ellender Duke

XX Wm Carter & Artimissi A. were **parents of Nora Louise (Lulu) Jones who married S. H. Lynch** and **Emma Irene Jones** who married **John Leland Allen.** Their son, **XX Leon H. Allen, Sr, married Estelle Vinson, granddaughter of J.A. Story and XX Their daughter, Mary Virginia Allen, married Geoffrey Lee Story, Jr.** grandson of Daniel Brooks Story.

XX 6) John C. b 1848 m. Sara Frances Story

Sara Frances was sister of Daniel Brooks and Alva Story, who married John's older sisters.

Interesting note: **XX7) Rebecca** married W. C. Morris, for whom Morris Chapel United Methodist Church was named.

LYNCH

Asbury Lynch

Born c. 1804 in Brunswick Va., 16th child of 34, Born to William Lynch & Eliza Grief (Wm. had 3 other wives), 2nd marriage to Eliz Duke in Jasper County, GA in 1836

2 children

1) William Herschel Lynch, 1838-1913
2) Sarah F. Lynch, 1841

1) XX Wm. Herschel pastored Hopewell 1875

9 children
 (1) M. O. Lynch
 (2) Rosalie Elzara
 (3) Nettie
 (4) **John Franklin**

Lambert, Orr, Vandiver, (B. Lindstrom), Quiggles, Irby, Grasso are all descendents from John Franklin.

    (5) James Asbury
    (6) D. B. (or J)
    (7) **Esther** m. Charlie Whatley, son Lynch, his children - Charles, Jim, Ernest, Esther, and Martha
    (8) **Schribner Herschel (Kim) (pastor 1901)**
       m. Nora Louise (Lulu) Jones (W. O.'s grandparents)
       Lulu was Emma Jones sister (Emma Jones was my father's mother)
    (9) **Wm. Arthur (pastor 1924/25)**

2) XX Sara b. 1841, m. James Wiley Story
<u>8 children</u>

    Simeon Hardy (See story about him)
    Wiley Asbury
    Mattie
    Wm. H
    Alonzo Drew
    Emma Tabitha
    Miranda
    Rilla

STORY

William Story Sr, b. before 1770 in N. C. Died in Pike, GA
Wife, Elizabeth

<u>6 children</u>
    1) **James B. Story** 1794 (NC)-1859 (Russell, now Lee, County) m. 3 times, 3rd wife, Ellender Duke
    2) Elizabeth
    3) David

4) Esther
5) **Wiley J.** – b c. 1807, m. Rebecca Beckham
6) **William, Jr.** 1809-1886, m Martha Beckham, possibly sister to Wiley's wife.

1) James B. Story
<u>7 children</u>
   1) Charlotte
   2) Sarah
   3) Daniel Floyd
   4) Asbury McCuin
   5) **XX Artimissi Antinette 1845-1927 m. William Carter Jones**
   6) Missouri Eunice
   7) **Judge Aaron** 1849-1922, m. Laura Jane Thomas - 6 children
      XX granddaughter Estelle Vinson m. Leon Allen, great grandson of William Carter Jones

5) Wiley J
<u>4 children</u>
   1) **XX James Wiley 1835-1901 m. Sara Lynch**
   2) Susan
   3) Delphia
   4) Emily

6) William, Jr.
<u>6 children</u>
   1) Elizabeth
   2) **XX Daniel Brooks 1836-1906 m. Elizabeth Jones**
      XX grandson, Geoffrey Lee Sr married Mary Allen, great granddaughter of William Carter Jones
   3) **XX Alva Silas m. Martha Ann Dudley Jones**
      Elizabeth and Martha, sisters of William Carter Jones, daughters of William Clayton Jones.

4) **XX Sara Frances b 1847, m. John C. Jones in Russell County. He was brother of Elizabeth, Martha and Wm. Carter, all of whom married Storys.**

5) Martha

6) Hiram

Memories Relatively Speaking

Talk given by Estelle V. Allen at
Jones-Lynch-Story Reunion, July 16, 2006

I am Estelle Vinson Allen, age 97, on August 31ST this year. Here's my birth certificate to prove I was born in 1909. I joined the church here at Hopewell in 1918. The old records will show that.

The old church, before this sanctuary was built, had oil lamps on the walls with reflectors. I wish at least one had been saved. There is an old beam or sill salvaged from the old church that stands at the entrance of the cemetery just behind the church. A bit of history saved there. The pews were not at all like the ones today. There was a 6" plank at seat level and another 6" plank above that. When there was a prayer, everyone knelt to pray. I remember as a small child I would open my eyes and peer through the opening in the back of the pew and see the backs of the people kneeling in prayer.

This sanctuary was built in 1925. There are records here at the church about collecting money for the building. My friend, Mildred Story, was one who is mentioned as a collector. Also mentioned is Mrs. D. P. Meadows (Cousin Gemmie). (Interesting thing Mama did not put in her talk was that Cousin Gemmie died teaching Sunday School at Hopewell in 1956.) John Lynch was Treasurer for the building fund. His brother, Rev. Arthur Lynch, was pastor. D. P. (Daniel Porter) Meadows supervised the building of the church. One of their daughters, Hazel M. Calhoun, told me she remembers going out on a rainy Sunday afternoon collecting money for the building.

Rev. W. H. Lynch conducted the funeral for one of James Story's sons, Daniel Floyd Story in 1885. D. F. Story was an "exhorter", not an ordained minister, but one who went about strongly urging people to live better lives.

"Miss" Arie Lynch once spent the night at our house in 1916. She was called a home missionary. That night before we went to bed, we all knelt down and she prayed with us.

In 1918, I remember Rev. S. H. "Kim" Lynch preaching a revival. I'm sure that one of those nights is when I joined the church. There is a membership roll that shows this. There were several others who joined at the same time. Two were my brother, Leland Vinson and Geoffrey Story.

I remember Mrs. Esther Lynch Whatley going by our house riding in a buggy with her daughter Fannie Mae on her way to Hopewell Church on a Saturday morning. At that time all business sessions were held on Saturday.

I also knew a younger member of the Lynch family. Herschel Lynch was at one time a missionary to Japan. Later, I met his wife. They lived in Sylacauga, I think.

James Story had three wives. The third wife was Ellender Duke. They had seven children. I knew five of them: Eunice, Antinette, Fannie, Nora and Judge Aaron, my grandfather.

William Clayton Jones is buried next to Daniel Brooks Story in the cemetery out back. I remember his son, William Carter Jones, (my Uncle Billy by marriage to my grandfather's sister, Artimissie Antinette Story). I also knew two of William Clayton Jones' daughters, one was Elizabeth who married Daniel Brooks Story and is buried at Hopewell, and Rebecca who married William C. Morris. They are buried at Morris Chapel, which was named for him. He was also the first pastor there. We have a copy of Uncle Billy's obituary which was written by Fannie Story Browning, his sister-in-law. She was very complimentary and said a lot of nice things about him.

****

2003 JLS Reunion

At the 2003 meeting, we acknowledged descendants of Obediah Story and John Franklin Lynch. Also, a human interest story about a **Story** was given concerning the disappearance of Simeon Hardy Story on December 16, 1875. Solved the mystery of what happened, but not the mystery of why...

Whatever Happened to **Simeon Hardy Story?**

Son of James Wiley Story and Sarah F. Lynch

September 16, 1858, **Simeon Hardy Story** was born in Lee County, AL.
April 1865 Civil war ended. Federal troops occupy the South. People struggle to survive. Children are an asset to a family by working in the fields and for extra income.
September 16, 1875, **Simeon** turns 17.
December 16, 1875, **Simeon Story** left home and was never heard from again. His mother, **Sarah Lynch Story**, in a letter dated June 16, 1877, writes, *"... for I have seen a lot of trouble for 2 or 3 years. Simeon leaving us caused me a great deal, almost more than I can bear and I never hear a word from him haven't since 16th of Dec. last, a year ago soon be 2 years. I have no hopes that he is living if only could hear from him what a pleasure it would be I try not to stude about him...."*

What we know and have proven:

Sept. 1, 1880, Simeon married Miss **Lenora N. Franks** in Cartersville, Bartow Co., GA. Cartersville is a major railroad terminal of northwest GA. Civil War battles were fought here for control of the railroad.
July 1881, a son, **James Alonzo**, was born in AL (per 1900 AL Census, Mobile Co. Ed 113, page 21, Line 27.)
On November 3, 1886, Simeon married **Alice Asaline Argo** of Dalton, GA in Hamilton Co., TN. From 1888-1896, they lived at Whistler, AL (today Prichard, AL) 5 miles north of Mobile, AL (The Daily

Register, April 11, 1897 "The Whistler City" column.) It was a major railroad town.

1897: **James Alonzo** was listed in the home of **S. H. Story**, 353 Eslava St., Mobile, AL in the 1897 City Directory. In the same directory, **Simeon H. Story** had a Fish and Oyster Restaurant at 310 Water St. **James A.** was a clerk for the business. **Simeon** was not listed after 1897. **Alonzo** was listed through 1913. He was called J. Alonzo, James A, in 1910. In 1911, he began working as a traveling salesman for Armour Co. Family history says he worked in Atlanta, Ga.

March, 1897, **Alice Krudop Story** was born to **Simeon and Alice Argo** in Mobile, AL.

April 9, 1897, **Alice Asaline Argo Story** died of chronic Nephritis. She was 29.

April 11, 1897, her service was held in Whistler Baptist Church and interment in Whistler Cemetery. (Daily Register, Mobile & Death Certificate). She was buried in Section C, SE ¼ of Square 5.

Simeon takes **Alice K. Story** to grandparents, **William Basil Argo** in GA to live (1900 Ga. Census, Whitfield Co. ED 105, page 35.) She grows up and remains there until she marries.

1900 Mississippi Census, Wayne Co., Beat 1 ED 109, page 16 List: **S. H. Story**, Widower and Carpenter., Same Census, page 15 List: **Hattie Stinson**

December 27, 1900, **Simeon** marries **Hattie L. Stinson** in Clark Co., MS.

1910 Mississippi Census, Forest Co., Beat 1, Hattiesburg, MS, **S. H. Story** and wife, **Hattie (Harriett L) Stinson**, Children : **Earnest** 7, **Edgar F.** 5, and **Lucille** 2.

August 18, 1913, **Lucille** dies with jaundice, impaction of gall duct. Buried at Oaklawn Cemetery, Hattisburg, MS

The flu epidemic of 1917 devastates **Simeon**'s family.

September 2, 1917, **Simeon** dies at Hattiesburg, MS. He is buried in Oaklawn Cemetery. Death Certificate indicates he was a traveling salesman for a Mill Supply House.

April 9, 1918, **James Earnest** dies in Meridian, MS (at grandfather Stinson's home) and is buried in Hattiesburg, MS.

1920 Mississippi Census, Forest Co., 708 Ryan S., Hattiesburg, MS lists: **Hattie**, widow, **Edgar** 14, **Hardy** 6 (**Simeon Hardy Story, Jr.**) and **Robert** 3.

August 13, 1920, **Hattie Stinson Story** dies at her father's (**S. S. Stinson**) home, Meridian, Lauderdale Co., MS. She is buried at Oaklawn Cemetery, Hattiesburg, MS with **Lucille, Earnest**, and **Simeon**.

Edgar, Hardy and Robert are placed in a Catholic Orphanage in Jackson, MS.

Edgar Fay Story – No records yet. He moved around. Worked as a brick mason out west. He may have died in the 1950's.

Simeon Hardy Story, Jr. applied for a SS # when he was 23 years old in Jackson, MS, on Jan 6, 1937. He was working at Jackson PTG. Co. 116 Roach St, Jackson, MS. His birthdate is July 27, 1913. He died July 15, 1994 in Polk Co, TX. He married three times. Had no children of his own. He raised **8 Glass stepchildren**. The Glass children say he was a great father! **S1, US Navy, WWII**

Robert Story (listed as **Storey** on his Social Security application, Born March 21, 1917, Hattiesburg, MS, died Jan. 26, 1987 in Denver CO. Was buried at Ft. Logan National Cemetery, Denver, CO., **Captain, US Army, WWII**. He may have descendants in the Denver area.

December 22, 1920, **James Alonzo Story** married **Louise Barksdale** in Fulton Co., GA. The marriage license listed her as **Mrs. Louise B. Story** which indicates she had been married to a Story. **Alonzo** worked for Armour Co. the rest of his life. They had no children. He died at home on May 6, 1952. He is buried at Crest Lawn Memorial Cemetery, Atlanta, GA.

Also at JLS Reunion, 2003

I regret that I did not find the copies of the reports given about **Obediah Sanford Story** and **John Franklin Lynch** at the 2003 reunion, because I am sure there was some human interest stories included as well as locations and other facts. Even so I am including a brief synopsis of information about them gleaned from **W. O. Lynch's 2000 Jones-Lynch-Story Families** booklet.

<u>**Obediah Sanford Story**</u> 1872-1944 was the son of **Daniel Brooks Story** 1836-1906 and **Elizabeth R. Jones** 1836-1905. His grandfather was **William Story, Jr.** 1809-1886. Siblings include: **Martha R.** 1859-1863, **Perry A.** 1861-1869, **Arilla Ellen** 1866-1943, **John Franklin** 1869-1946, **Laura E.** 1874-, **Uriah Lee** 1877-1941.

His wife was **Ella Hymonia Corbitt** 1870-1921. His children were **Mary Exa** 1896-, **Elsie Behethlon** 1898-, **Lilla** 1900 -, **Jimmie Alma** 1901-, **Alice Rebecca** 1904 -, **Leroy Sanford** 1906-, **Ella Jewel** 1909-1977.

Some family names of his descendants are: **Quattlebaum, Hicks, Herring, Filar, Watts, Joiner, Wilkerson, Benefield, Parker, Thornton, Vanwyck and Metcalf.**

****

<u>**John Franklin Lynch**</u> 1867-1940 was the son of **William Herschel Lynch** 1838-1913 and **Jemima Frances Bentley** 1842-1915.He and his first wife, **Mary Belle Allen** 1871-, had 7 children: **Carl Houston** 1901-1955, **Mildred Olivia** 1903-1908, **Lewis Allen** 1905-1965, **John DeLance** 1907-1972, **Lola Ruth** 1909-1997, **Elsie Elizabeth** 1912-, **Mary Cumi** 1917-1989. He and his second wife had 5 children: **Amanda** 1889-1889, **Pheddie Eldridge** 1889-1947, **Essie Irene** 1892-1977, **James Asbury** 1895-1962, **Julia Eugenia** 1897-1969.

Family names of descendants include: **Lambert, Garland, Champ, Nichols, Orr, Lindstrom, Quiggle, Grasso, Riddle, Irby, Williams, Stribling, Rochester, Startley, Underwood and Morgan.**

July 17, 2004 Reunion

William Arthur Lynch
By Rev. Wesley Otis Lynch, Jr.
(Great nephew)

W. O. prepared a wonderful report and handout filled with genealogy lists, Bible records, pictures and Lynch Clan information as far back as the Colony of Virginia. More specifically, although we do not know how they were related, three Linch men are known to have owned land in Brunswick County, VA. Descendants believe that **Thomas Linch** was the father and **John** and **William (1)** were his sons. We are fairly certain that **William Linch (1)** and **Rachel Steed** had a son named William, whom we believe was William, Sr., the name used in an 1827 Virginia General Assembly Act on his behalf. **William, Sr.** named a daughter, **Rachel Steed Lynch**. This ties him to **William Linch (1)** who married **Rachel Steed**.

The 1827 Virginia General Assembly on February 9, 1827, passed an Act exempting **William Lynch, Sr.** from payment of public or county tax. It was noted that he was the father of thirty-four legitimate children, of which twenty-seven were still living; and that he had been the husband of four wives. Some family stories say that three wives had 10 children each and one wife had 4. W. O. listed the names of 24 children: **Adin, Sion, Syrach, Laxton, Viney, Claxton, Jarratt, Greif, Gray, Mary Harmon, Meredith, Lemuel, Chancy, Edlow, Gilbert G., Aggy Barefoot, Asbury, Rachel Steed, Nancy Clack, Joseph A., Benjamin W., William Lynch, Jr., Faith Coleman**, and **James H.**

We believe his first wife's name was **Eliza Grief**, second is **unknown**, third was **Nancy Wright**, and fourth was **Eliza Lynch**. He was a **Patriot in 1776** and provided beef for the army.

In his Will of January 1, 1833, **William Lynch, Sr.**, of Brunswick County, Virginia, names twenty-two children. The Will is written is such a way that would indicate that these are all of the living or deceased children with heirs. **William Lynch, Sr.** probably died between January and August of 1837. A study of Censuses and age of children indicated he was born between 1748 and 1750.

Asbury Lynch was **William Arthur Lynch**'s grandfather. He was the son of **William Sr.**'s third marriage of October 25, 1802 to **Nancy Wright**. In 1829, he moved to Morgan County, Georgia, to live near or with his brothers, **Grief, Gilbert G., and Edlow** as he paid Poll Tax there for the years of 1829-1830. On December 4, 1832, **Asbury** married **Ann Johnston**, daughter of **Hollan Warren** and **Bartholomew Johnston** in Morgan County, Georgia. In 1835, his wife Ann died at the birth of a daughter. The daughter was living in 1840 in Asbury's home, but we do not know her name or what happened to her.

Asbury married **Elizabeth Duke*** on January 5, 1836, in Jasper County, Georgia. They were married by his nephew, **Ephriam Lynch**, a Justice of the Peace and son of **Grief Lynch**. May 16, 1838, Bartholomew Johnston died and **Asbury** signed as an heir with his mark (**X**). It was also in 1835 that **Asbury**'s father's Will left him $1.00.

The 1840 Census shows Asbury to be 30-40 years of age. His wife is 20-30. Ann's daughter is 5-10 and a son, **William Herschel,** is 1-5 years of age. The last written record of Asbury is when he appears before the Jasper County Inferior Court to give an appraisal for a horse on June 8, 1841.

Asbury and **Elizabeth Duke** had a second child, **Sarah Frances Lynch**, in 1841 or 1842. According to family letters, **Asbury** died before 1850. The family was in Troup or Harris County Georgia. We do not know where **Asbury** is buried. He could be buried by his first wife in Morgan County, Georgia, or in a Jasper county cemetery, where his brother, **Grief**, is buried.

*Note by Annette Edwards: (Interestingly, it is thought by some members of the Story family that **Elizabeth Duke** was the sister of **Ellender Duke** who was the third wife of **James B. Story** as she, too, was from Jasper County, Georgia.)

On December 18, 1858, **Sarah Frances Lynch** married **James Wiley Story**, in Russell County (now Lee), Alabama. She was 14 years old. In

1860, **William Herschel Lynch** received land from the Government. On September 15, 1861, **William Herschel** married **Jemima Frances Bentley**, daughter of **Jeremiah Franklin Bentley**, a preacher involved in starting and dedicating **Hopewell Methodist Protestant Church**. Jemima was the spiritual force that led to two of their sons, **William Arthur** and **Scribner Herschel**, becoming Methodist preachers and a daughter, **Rosalie Elzara** to marry a preacher, **Wesley Crawford Jackson**.

William Herschel had a cankerous sore on his leg that plagued him all his life. It prevented him from serving in the Civil War. Some think he also had polio. One story is that he had a toddy of whiskey each day for the sore. When prohibition came in, he stopped taking the sip and died. He apparently was a good farmer as he eventually had several hundred acres of land. Each year he would mortgage his land to make a crop. His farm was equipped with a blacksmith shop. An old store record shows that he traded nails and hinges he made for goods. He also ran a store.

His grandchildren said he was a gentle and loving person. They loved to visit him. Jemima was more of a disciplinarian and they watched their "p's and q's" when around her.

William Herschel Lynch and wife

They were strong supporters of Hopewell Church. The visiting preachers often ate and stayed with them. Their children were raised with a good religious background. Their life centered around farm work and church. Church at that time was a weekly social event. In old age, they stayed with their daughter, **Esther Cumi** and her husband, **Charlie Whatley.**

William Arthur Lynch was the youngest son of **William Herschel Lynch** and **Jemima Frances Bentley.** Arthur's early life was helping on the farm and attending church. He joined Hopewell Church when he was 12 years old. On December 24, 1899, he married his first wife **Lilla Vesta Phillips.** Due to death, he married two more times to **Bertha Susanna Lochenhour Evans** and **Nancy Lou Hearn Montgomery.**

W. H. Lynch Homestead
William Arthur, Alywun Hershell, Lilla Vesta Phillips, William Herschel, Jemima Frances Bentley
1901

Lynch family

Arthur was licensed to preach by the Methodist Protestant Church, Lee Circuit, Alabama, in 1900 by J.L. Mosley, Pastor. In 1903, he joined the Alabama Methodist Protestant Conference. On November 14, 1911, he received his License to Administer the Ordinances. He had met the requirement to allow him to serve Communion and perform marriages. By May 31, 1912, he was Ordained and given Elder's Credentials as a member of the Methodist Protestant Conference at The Bibb Street Methodist

Protestant Church in Montgomery, Alabama. Rev. J. P. Morgan was President and Ira Champion, Treasurer.

Following is his record of service:

Church/Circuit	Year	Church/Circuit	Year
Chilton	1903-1905	Lee	1924-1925
Jefferson	1906	Coosa	1926-1927
Tuscaloosa	1907-1909	Wilcox	1928-1930
Clark	1910	Mt. Carmel	1931-1934
China Grove	1911-1912	Shelby	1935-1936
Georgiana	1913-1916	Weogufka	1937-1938
Pike	1917-1919	Wilsonville	1939-1940
Tuscaloosa	1920-1921	Helena	1941-1942
Superannuated (Sick)	1922	Leeds	1943-1944
Georgiana	1923		

Arthur Lynch

Uriah Lee Story ((1877-1941)
Spotlight Family JLS Reunion 2006

Given by Kenneth Story

Uriah Lee Story was the son of **Daniel Brooks Story** and **Elizabeth B. Jones** (both of whom are buried in the Hopewell Cemetery), the grandson of **William Story, Jr.** and **Martha (also called Patsie) Beckham Story,** and the great-grandson of **William Story, Sr.,** and **Elizabeth.** William, Sr.'s parents (or grandparents) are thought to have come from Ireland.

William, Jr. was born in North Carolina, lived in Pike County, GA, and later moved to what is now Lee County, AL, where he died.

Daniel Brooks Story married **Elizabeth B. Jones** in the **William Clayton Jones** home in the Hopewell area. He served in the Confederate Army and was taken prisoner, from best we can tell at Mission (maybe Missionary) Ridge in November 1863 and was released at Rock Island, Illinois, June 20, 1865. **Daniel B.** and **Elizabeth** had seven children, of which **Uriah Lee** (called **Lee**) was the youngest. The other children were **Martha R., Perry A., Arrilla Ellen** (who married **James M. Parker**), **John Franklin** (who married **Panola Ann Scott**, sister of **Lee**'s wife **Henrietta Scott**), **Obadiah Sanford** (who married **Ella Hymonia Corbitt**), and **Laura E.** (who married **George Henry Parker**, brother of **James M. Parker**, married to her sister, **Arilla**).

Lee Story was first married to **Odessa** L. According to the Census of 1900, they were living with **Daniel B. and Elizabeth** in the Pierce Chapel precinct of Lee County. Shortly after the Census, **Odessa** died in August, 1900.

The Lee and Etta story begins with their marriage on September 1, 1906. They will have nine children. Seven of their children will live to adulthood.

Lee and Etta Story

Lee Story married **Henrietta (Etta) Scott** on September 1, 1906, in LaFayette, AL. In the 1920 Census, they are recorded as living at Graham's Store in Lee County. Seven children have been born to them: **William Brooks (W. B.), Mildred Vasti, Geoffrey Lee, Woodrow Wilson** (who only lived 23 months), **Josephine Elizabeth, Andrew Cyril, and Owen Horace**. By the Census of 1930, two more children have been born: **Henrietta Inez** and **Marie Antionette** (who only lived 1-1/2 years).

In researching records, we found that **Lee Story** was an active member of Hopewell church, participating in Sunday School classes, serving as a Class Leader, Trustee, and on the Board. Daughter **Mildred** helped raise money in 1925 for a new church building and in 1930 for a new piano. She played the piano for the church from 1925 until she moved to Columbus, Ga. She, **Josephine, Henrietta**, and sister in law, **Mary Allen Story**, were members of the Missionary Society in the 1930's. **Geoffrey** remained a faithful member throughout his life. One of the memories mentioned of him was his bringing the tub of ice for all the dinner meetings (including JLS Reunions) for the ladies to pour their Southern Sweet Tea over and then standing by to serve it up. **Mildred** served as secretary of JLS reunions until her death.

Lee's and **Etta's** children went on to a variety of careers. Four of them were involved in education: **W. B.** as a county agent in Sumter County, AL, for 33 years, **Mildred** as a teacher with her longest tenure as a first grade teacher at Ridgon Road School in Columbus, GA, for 19 years, and **Josephine and Henrietta** as Home Economics teachers in Oneonta, AL and Mobile, AL, respectively. **Geoffrey and Andrew** were businessmen in Lee County with a number of interests. Meadows Mill and the Meadows Mill Grocery were a large part of **Geoffrey**'s life, and **Andrew**'s business, Story's on Geneva Street in Opelika continues with his son **Andy** as proprietor. **Owen**'s longest career was his service of our country in the U. S. Army. All except Mildred married and had children and Mildred was the kind of Aunt that every child should have.

We have heard that **Lee** was married a third time, but have not documented that. He died on August 24, his birthday, in 1941, in an accident and is buried in the Hopewell Cemetery.

****

William Carter Jones - Parents, Siblings and Descendants

For JLS Reunion. July 19th, 2008
By Lucy Annette Allen Edwards

William Carter Jones was born to *William Clayton Jones* and his wife, *Rebecca Beheathlan Lassiter* on April 24, 1845, in Hopewell community, Russell County, Alabama. I read somewhere in my notes that Rebecca's mother's maiden name was Beheathland and there were no sons to carry on the family name, so they named her Beheathlan. *William Clayton* and *Rebecca* had ten children. An educated guess is that they moved from Pike, Georgia, in 1842. William Carter's three older sisters were all born in Pike, GA, but brother just 2 years older than he, (4) *Robert Isaac*, was born in 1843 in Russell County.

First, let's talk about the siblings of my great grandfather, *William Carter Jones* (or *Uncle Billy*, as my mother called him, since his wife was a sister to my mother's grandfather, *Judge Aaron Story* —see next report).

His oldest sister, (1) *Elizabeth R Jones*, was born in Pike County, GA, on January 5, 1838, and was married to *Daniel Brooks Story*, son of

William Story, Jr., in the *William Clayton Jones* home in the Hopewell community on December 9, 1857. *Daniel Brooks Story's* parents, *William Story, Jr.* and *Martha Beckham* married in 1835 in Pike County, GA, so the Story's must have moved to this area about the same time as the Joneses. *William Carter* was 12 years old when they got married. Two of their seven children, were recently spotlighted at our reunion: *Obadiah* in 2003 and *Uriah Lee* in 2006.

In 1860, a sister, (3) *Martha Ann Dudley Jones*, married *Alva Silas Story*, a brother to *Daniel Brooks Story*. They had 5 children. I met their great granddaughter, *Mary Ann Hydrick*, as a teenager at a MYF meeting in Auburn. I wish I had kept in touch. I went to school at Beauregard with some other great granddaughters, *Janice, Marian, Zelda and Betty Grace Edwards*. They had 2 older brothers, *James and Milo*, but I did not know them.

Later, a younger brother, (6) *John C. Jones*, would marry a sister of Daniel Brooks Story, *Sara Frances Story*. We know they had 5 children, but are not sure where they lived or where their descendants are now. We think they moved to Texas. Mama said it was generally thought that they moved out of the country.

It is widely thought that the Story's can be traced back to 1770 in North Carolina. *William Story, Sr.* and his wife, *Elizabeth*, moved to Pike, GA, after the birth of their 6 children. Their youngest son, William, Jr. was born in 1809 in North Carolina. At least 3 of their 4 sons, *James B., Wiley J., and William Jr.* moved on to Russell County, Alabama (now Lee County). The date is uncertain, but the youngest was married in Pike, Ga. in 1835 before moving on to Alabama. The two youngest possibly married sisters as both their last names were Beckham. *James*, who was the oldest, was married to his third wife in June, 1836. Her name was **Ellender Duke**. Her sister, *Elizabeth Duke*, was 2nd wife to *Asbury Lynch*. <u>Asbury and Elizabeth</u> were married in Georgia in January, 1836. Records show that James went back to Georgia to get his third bride as he had done for his first two. (Perhaps Elizabeth and Asbury told him about her.) He had married his first two wives in Harris Country, GA, according to Harris County records.

(There are conflicting records as to whether this is the correct lineage for the *James Story* that married *Ellender Duke*. Library of Congress records indicate my ancestor *James Story* who definitely WAS married to *Ellender Duke* was a son of *James Story* and *Esther Wilson*. The elder *James Story* was the son of *Daniel Story*, a revolutionary war naval officer from Southhampton County, VA. I've tried to tie the two lineages together, but so far without success.)

Back to the *Jones* family. The next to oldest sister, (2) *Mary Arilla Jones* married *Andrew J Ruffin*, but no more is known about them.

(4) *Robert Isaac Jones*, sibling just older than William Carter, married *Nancy Ballard Blalock* and they had 5 children. No more is known about them.

After (5) *William Carter* came (6) *John C.*, whom we have already mentioned. Since he married a member of the Story family, it is surprising that we do not know more about them.

Another sister, (7) *Rebecca J. Jones* was born in 1849. She married *William C. Morris*. Morris Chapel Church was named for him. They are buried in Morris Chapel Cemetary. Their son, *Olin Morris* was our rural mail carrier when I was young. He was married to *Florence Jones*, a descendant from the Joneses on my mother's side of the family. Her father was a younger half-brother to *DeKalb Jones*, whose daughter, **Lucy Jones Vinson** (my first name is Lucy), is my namesake and my mother's father's mother. Their daughter is *Frances Morris Walton*, who lives in Opelika.

Nothing is known about the 3 youngest brothers, (8) *L. O. Jones*, (9) *T. C. Jones*, and (10) *G. A. Jones*, other than *T. C.* was married to a woman named *Mary Harvey*.

Finally, we get to (5) *William Carter*. He married a Story, cousin to the Story's married by 3 of his siblings. Her name was *Artimissie Antinette Story*, and she was a sister to my mother's grandfather on her mother's side. (picture of William Carter and Antinette below)

William Carter and Artimissi Antinette

Keep in mind that *William Carter* and *Antinette* are my father's grandparents. So my great grandmother was also my great aunt. Oh what a twisted web we find when we study the Jones/Story background. This is one of the great grandmother's I was named after, just with a slight variation in the spelling of the name.

Grandpa Billy (1845-1919) and *Grandma Nette* (1845-1927) were married in 1869, according to W. O.'s genealogy. They had 6 children. They were *Floyd, Emma Irene, William Seaborn, Nora Louise, Zippora Fair*, and *Andrew Valentine*. Since their second child, *Emma Irene* was born in 1869, the year they were married, and we have no date information on *Floyd*, perhaps he was actually born after Emma, even though W.O's genealogy lists him first. Very little is known about *Zippora* and *Andrew*. I have heard some people speak of *Aunt Zip* and *Andrew* is mentioned as a Methodist Protestant Itinerant (or traveling preacher) in *William Carter's* obit. Anyway, today we will focus on *Emma Irene, William Seaborn* and *Nora Louise*.

William Carter and *Artimissie Antinette* are buried side by side in Hopewell cemetery. A glowing tribute to *William Carter Jones* was written for the Alabama Methodist Protestant Christian Advocate by his wife's sister, *Mrs. Fannie Browning*. She writes that he died May 31, 1919, at the age of 74. He and his *Antinette* joined the Methodist Protestant Church at Hopewell at the same time in 1860. He served his country under the Confederate flag during the Civil War. Mrs. Browning said: "He has not an enemy in the world." And "His church was his pride." She also complimented his patience and Christian fortitude.

(A)*Emma Irene Jones Allen* (1869 - 1925) was my father's mother. She had three children: *Sarah Kate Allen Hinson, Leon Hartwell Allen, Sr.,* and *Mary Virginia Allen Story*. I understand that she was a very hard person and a very strict parent. Perhaps this was because her children were born late in her life. She was 40 when she had her first child and 45 when her youngest was born. (Actually she was married before to a Stripling and had two babies, neither of which lived. This could have caused extreme sadness.) She married a very handsome man when she married Mr. Allen. Two cousins, my sister, one of my daughters, one granddaughter, and one great grandson inherited her red hair. Daddy used to tell us children that when he was a child and there were guests for a meal, the children were told to take a "cold tater" and wait. He said usually there wasn't much left but chicken gizzards, livers or wings for the children to eat. My father was about 13 or 14 years old when his mother died of tuberculosis at 56. *Emma Irene* is buried beside my grandfather, *John Leland Allen*, in Hopewell cemetery even though he was married to his third wife at his death. *Mr. Allen* married two more times, but the relationship between his wives and his children was not especially good. All three children remained faithful to Hopewell Church until their deaths. They also remained very close all their lives. My father was a very special person. He was a very intelligent person. He was very fair and had the most common sense of any person I have ever known. He loved his family and made a good living for us. His love and patience was very evident as my mother's mother came to live with us when I was 10 and my grandfather died. Grandma, **Laura Olivia Story Vinson**, was about 65 at the time and she lived with us until her death at 96. I never heard him say a negative word about their having to take care of her. In fact I never heard him say a bad word. Even when he scolded us children, he never raised his voice. My mother's statement about my father: "I married **Leon Hartwell Allen, Sr**, on January 20, 1935. He was a good husband, a good father, a good friend, a good Christian and a good member of Hopewell Church." In June, 1985, Daddy was very emotional. Knowing that **Aunt Sarah** lay dying in the hospital in Columbus, GA, I heard him say to those attending this reunion that year that he felt that he would be next to go. He lasted until October. His favorite hymn was "Wonderful Words of Life" and he often requested that we sing that hymn. I used to love to go to **Aunt Sarah**'s to play with my cousin, **Lurline**, even though **Uncle Luther** always pulled his pocket knife out and threatened to cut off my ears! I was always careful to steer clear of him and keep someone between us! I loved their home and the stained glass in the front door. For a while when I was young, daddy and **Uncle Geoffry**, **Aunt Mary**'s husband owned Meadows' grist mill and store together. Once I was keeping the store and a country fella' came in to buy his lunch. He asked for some "mo" meat. I asked him what kind he had gotten before. Turns out there was a brand of canned meat called Mor, spelled MOR and that is what he wanted.

I could talk all day about the good times we had and the wonderful relationship our family had with Daddy's sisters and their families. We had an annual **Allen** Christmas Party. We would go to a different sibling's home each year. **Kenneth**, **Aunt Mary's** son, and his wife **Carol Meadows Story** have kept the tradition alive by hosting the event for the last few years.

B) *William Seaborn Jones* (1870-1950). *Uncle Seab* was married to *Emily Hester Cadenhead*. She was a sister to *Sultana Cadenhead Story*, who was my great grandfather's second wife. I knew *Sultana* as my *Grandma Story*. She was my *Grandma Ollie Story Vinson*'s stepmother and was a good mother to her step children and her children. *William Seaborn* was a Methodist Protestant minister. I remember seeing him and *Aunt Hester* a number of times when I was a young girl. They had four children, all girls. *Katie*, their first, died at the age of 3. *Nettie Myrtle* lived to be 93 years old. She married *Lee Roy Coggins.* Their granddaughter, *Barbara "Faye" Coggins Tankersly* and her husband of 39+ years, *Jimmy Tankersly*, usually attend our reunions. One of her brothers is an ordained minister in the Presbyterian church. *William Seaborn*'s next daughter, *Mildred Elizabeth Jones,* lived to be 94. She married *James Clause Simms* and their daughter, *Mildred "Millie" Nancy Sims Peters* comes to reunion when she can. *Willie Clara Jones* married *William Albert Salter*. Their daughter, *Billie Elizabeth Salter Atkinson*, who also comes when she can is attending her only grandchild's first birthday celebration this weekend.

C) *Nora Louise Jones* (1873-1922). In some ways, *Nora Louise*, or *"Lula"* as she was called, is the possibly the most interesting of *William Carter Jones*' children, although she died quite young, at just 49 years of age. She was a member of Hopewell Church and was smitten by *Scribner Herschel Lynch*, better known as *"Kim"* when he pastored at Hopewell in 1901-1902. *"Kim"* was born during his father's ministry at Hopewell in 1875 and lived here until his father was moved to another church in 1878. Before he died, *W. O.* gave me some copies of some of their correspondence during their courtship after "*Kim*" was moved to another church in 1903. *Lula* and *Kim* are buried in Hopewell Cemetery in the same grave. *Kim* died in November, 1921, and *Lula* died in March, 1922. They had six children: *Edward Herschel, Wesley Otis, Sr, Andrew Gladys, Nettie Thelma, John Curtis and Eva Mae*. Their oldest and youngest sons both died the year they were born. *Wesley Otis, Sr.* was called *Otis*. *Otis* had 3 children, *Catherine Phoenell, W. O, Jr.*, and *Joseph Schribner. Hansons. Dannhausers or Gingles* represent Otis's oldest child. *Wesley Otis, Jr.*, whom we knew fondly as *W. O.*, was the most well-known descendant to all of us. He was the most prominent figure involved in helping to recapture the reunion in 2000, after several years of our not getting together. And it is his genealogy record from which I get many names and dates to use in my talks! We are still mourning his death in 2005. I have heard of **Gladys Lynch** as **Andrew Gladys** was known, but I do not remember him. I do remember that some of his descendents names have been on our mailing lists over the years, namely, **Valorie Page, Carol Mills, Wally Lynch, Becky Montgomery, Jane Rusth, John Builta and Martha Williams. Kathryn Frye** and her husband, **Michael**, who live in Fresno, CA, are the only descendents of **Nettie Thelma Lynch** and **William Edgar Williams** that are on our mailing list. **Eva May Lynch** was only 11 years old when her father died and only 12 when her mother, **"Lula"**, died. **Otis** and his wife, **Josie**, cared for **Eva Mae** until she grew up. **Eva Mae** married **Frank Herman Alverdes** and they had two sons, **Walter Lynch** and **Richard Emil. Richard** and his wife **Teri** are with us here today all the way from the sate of Washington. I asked all of you with help for this program and for the display table. I got some help from several people with dates and names for the genealogy, but **Richard** is the only one who shared a story for me to tell. Here it is in **Richard**'s words, (and I hope you can understand it as I read what you said, **Richard**):

"What Didja Say?"

"Mom always looked forward to going to the reunions, but I did not cherish her leaving. Now, you must understand that I did not regret her going for she truly loved every aspect of it and the opportunities to visit with her family and many friends, but it was when mom came home that I had the most trouble. Mom lived in the Pacific Northwest for many years and she lost her "Southern Accent", but when she came home from the South, she returned to her natural "Southern Drawl", and for the life of me, I could not understand most of what she was saying. It was really funny, for I never was exposed to the inflection and pronouncement of words like she would use and I would have to ask her to repeat words many times over. Simple words, like my name for example. "Richard" had a new meaning when I heard it right after she returned or the word "Wash" was truly different. Mom and I would laugh a lot and I would try to say them like her, but they never came out right. Mom would call me a "Northerner" and I called her a "Southerner". When I joined the US Navy and left home, we continued our "battle of words" but shifted it to the annual football game between "Navy" and "Alabama". Of course *Eva Mae* always took Alabama and I rooted for the Navy. That was a tough task for Mom, for she was not into football, but she never missed the opportunity to keep our "North versus South" rival going.

****

Judge Aaron's Story

Prepared by Annette Allen Edwards
For Jones Lynch Story Reunion, 2010

Today, our spotlight is on my great grandfather, **Judge Aaron Story**. Two years ago I talked about another great grandfather of mine, **William Carter Jones**. Perhaps I could have rolled the two together and just talked about my great grandmother, **Artimissie Antinette Story Jones**. Since she was the wife of **William Carter Jones** and the sister of **Judge Aaron Story**, I could have covered them all at the same time. But then I would have talked at only one reunion… and what would we have done today?

I want to acknowledge that much of the information I used to prepare this tale today came from my mother, **Estelle Vinson Allen** and her mother, **Laura Olivia Story Vinson**.

Two amazing young women in Spartanburg County got together for prayer and coffee over the past year and ended up writing a Bible Study based on the life of Noah. They share a common bond due to illness in their families, but they also share a strong faith in God to see them through their trials. One lost her teen aged daughter to cancer soon after she graduated high school. The other has four children, three of which are afflicted with a genetic disease and have to go to far off cities for surgery from time to time. One child has already had three surgeries.

I am privileged to be participating in their first class of study. Their stories and their faith are inspiring. They claim their study of Noah could not start with Noah, but had to start with "In the Beginning", so we started at Genesis Chapter 1, verse 1.

In the same way my talk about Judge Aaron would not be complete without some background ancestors. So:

Through my recent forays into the website www.ancestry.com, I have learned that **Judge Aaron Story**'s ancestry can be traced back seven generations of Storys to **Edward Story** born in England about 1625. His wife was named **Sarah**. I was also able to find that we can trace even further back through **Judge Aaron**'s great great grandmother's side of the family. Her name was **Sarah Jenkins**. Her mother's maiden name was **Skelderman** and her grandmother's maiden name was **Norton**. Eight generations back from **Judge Aaron**, **George Gravely** was born in Offaly County, Ireland in 1580. He came to the US before 1740 because his daughter, **Letitia**, married **Lucas Norton** in 1740 in Virginia. **Lucas** was born in Bedforshire, England of English parents, **Thomas Norton** (8 generations back from **Judge Aaron**) and **Elizabeth Marshall**. **Elizabeth**'s father was **Robert Marshall** (9 generations back). He was born in Hampshire, England around 1554. Add 3 **generations to all that if you are counting from me! That makes it 10, 11 and 12 generations ago for me! It is very interesting how many generations of the name James Story** there were (5) and how many of the **Story** men married a woman named **Sarah** (3)!

On January 5, 1956, my grandmother, **Ollie Vinson**, wrote some notes about her family. Later, my mother blended those with more information she had. What I am about to read to you is a mixture of both of those renderings with the addition of my own notes. We will start with information about **Judge Aaron**'s father, **James B. Story**. He was born in Mecklenburg County, NC on May 4, 1794. His great grandfather, also named **James** was born in Virginia, but moved to North Carolina around 1750. After his birth, the first record we have of **James B. Story** is from Oglethorpe County, GA. His name is also in records in Pickens County and later in Harris County, GA. His first marriage was to **Elizabeth**

Lambert on Sept 18, 1818. They had 5 children….. After her death, James married **Matilda Downs** in 1832. They had 2 children…. They moved into the Indian country of Russell County, Alabama in 1834. **Matilda** died in 1835. On June 8, 1836, **James**, along with one of his daughters by his first marriage, **Elizabeth**, returned to Harris County, Georgia, on horseback to the home of Captain **William and Mary Green Duke** near Flat Rock Creek Church to be married to their daughter, **Ellender** (known as **Ellen**). This is her story: **James** was wearing a linen suit upon arrival on horseback. He asked if he should change his suit for the wedding. Thinking perhaps he had a nicer suit, she said, "I believe I would." She told that she was a little embarrassed when he came out in a little checked homespun suit. **Ellen** wore a white dotted Swiss dress with a black silk scarf. She was known to be very pretty with fair skin and very blue eyes. After the wedding, they rode back to his large one room house in Russell County, Alabama. Now can you imagine taking a new bride on horseback to a one room house when he already has seven children? Must not have bothered them much. They went on to have 9 children of their own! Anyway, early the next morning, he wanted her to go with him to see his beautiful field of corn. Some years later, he built a larger house of hewn logs. By larger, I mean a two room house. Of course, there was a kitchen out back and two covered porches. This farm was located in Township 18, Section 24, Range 27, less than a mile from here. This log house was torn down in about 1958. A mill pond was built in 1840. (My mother, who was born in 1909, remembers going to that pond as a child.) Their 9 children were: **Charlotte, Lucinda, Daniel, Asbury, Antinette, Eunice, Judge Aaron, Leonora,** and **Frances.**

I want to do a little aside here on **Ellender Duke**'s family. Obviously she is not in the direct **Story** line, but she was **Judge Aaron**'s mother! While on ancestry.com, I also learned that **Ellen Duke**'s mother's name was probably not just **Mary** as we had always thought, but **Mary Elizabeth Green**. Capt. **William Duke**'s father was a **Cpl. William Duke** in the Revolutionary War in NC near the VA border. He lived to be 80 years old. **Mary Elizabeth** was his first wife. My grandmother, **Ollie Story Vinson**, only knew 3 sisters names and one half-brother's name. She did not realize that he was a half- brother. Anyway, it seems that **Capt. Duke** who died at

69, had 3 wives and 22 children! His first wife had 8 children, including **Ellen**. She died at 39, probably giving childbirth. His second wife, **Polly Harris**, died at 32 after having 5 children. His 3rd wife lived 54 years and had 9 children. There is some indication that there was a 4th wife, who outlived him by 2 years. **Ellen** was his 3rd child and did not get married until she was 27, the year after her youngest half-siblings birth. Guess she was experienced in childcare! Now remember she married **James B. Story** who had 7 children and then had 9 of her own and still lived to be 91 years old! She lived 42 years after her husband died at age 65.

James and Ellen were charter members of Hopewell Methodist Protestant Church which was established in 1846. They are buried in the church cemetery as well as six of their children, namely **Lucinda, Daniel, Artimissie Antinette, Judge Aaron, Leonora**, and **Frances**. You will find **Judge Aaron**'s slab up near the church with a fresh cemetery floral arrangement on it.

Lucinda married **Newton Martin**. They had 10 children. One was named **Cooper**. He became a Methodist minister.

Antinette married **William Carter Jones**, my great grandfather on my father's side of the family. Two of their sons became Methodist ministers, **William Seaborn** and **Andrew Valentine**. One daughter, **Nora Louise (Lula)** married a Methodist minister **S. H. (Kim) Lynch**. Lulu and Kim had 4 children, two of whom were also ministers.

Daniel (Dock), a licensed exhorter, married **Frances Thomas** who was a first cousin to **Laura Jane Thomas**, first wife of **Judge Aaron.**

WOW! We finally get to **Judge Aaron**! **Judge Aaron** married twice, first to **Laura Jane Thomas**, daughter of **William Thomas**, better known as **Bill**. They had six children: **Louanna Estelle** married **John Crawford Ledbetter**, the son of a Methodist preacher. They raised 5 children, **Joseph Luther, Rosa Virginia, Corene, James V.** and **Thomas Aaron**. Two of **Luther**'s children became ministers. **Bob Casaday** shared a memory of picking cotton with his **Papa Ledbetter (Luther)**. He remembers how hard it was to lean over and pick the cotton bolls even at a young age.

He recalls how he would pick a couple of rows standing and leaning over, then pick a couple of rows on his knees. He would soon be left behind as the others picked way ahead of him. My guess is he started to daydream and lag on purpose…. Even when he was a young man, his grandfather could pick 200# a day, but he could never muster more than 150# a day. I remember that most every year as I was growing up, **Aunt Louanna** and **Uncle Crawford** would come to visit us. **Aunt Louanna** spent a lot of time crocheting and she was very good at it. I was fascinated that she used snuff and that no one seemed to mind. Of course if you look carefully at **Great Great Grandmother Ellen**'s picture you will see that she is holding a corncob pipe, so I assume she smoked it! The picture below is thought to be made in 1900 when she was 90 years old.

Ellender Duke Story

Eugene Dorsey, Judge Aaron's second child, married **Georgie Killibrew**. They had two daughters: **Roma Irene** and **Mildred**. I have wonderful memories of **Uncle Dorsey** coming to visit us over the years. I am sure we had the visits from these great uncles and aunts because my grandmother lived with us. Sometimes he brought his grandson, **Bobby MacGregor** with him. He usually spent more time with my brother shooting firecrackers and such in later years, but I remember when **Judge Aaron**'s second wife **Sultana** was still alive playing outside her house with Bobby. One particular memory is of chasing the chickens with sticks that were on fire! I really don't think it was my idea, but I was all for it as I remember. **Uncle Dorsey** was a railroad man and helped build the railroad down the east coast of Florida. He lived in St. Augustine, FL, in 1920, near some of **Charles Sykes'** ancestors according to my sister, **Lenora**. **Lenora** and her husband **Charles** have done a lot of ancestry study of their own. My brother, **Hartwell**, can tell you many more good stories about **Uncle Dorsey** and others. He was a very attentive young man when our uncles and aunts visited and told stories.

Laborn Morgan was a music lover. He died as a young man and never married.

Nettie Willa married **Eugene Riddle**. (Wedding party pictured below: L to right, front row: Laura Olivia Story, Eugene Dorsey Story, Viola Riddle. Back Row, Odessa Riddle Story, Willa Story Riddle, Eugene Riddle, Morgan Story, Lala Riddle Thomas. Circa 1900)

Wedding party

They raised 3 children: **Gladys, Poleman** and **Mattie Bruce**. I have a memory of visiting **Mattie Bruce** in Opelika as a teenager with my grandmother. **Gladys**'s daughter, **Janelle**, who was about my age was also visiting her. We spent almost all day in the hot sun playing tennis. First time I had sun poisoning! When we came inside we kept washing our faces with cold water over and over.

On Dec. 21, 1903, **Laura Olivia (Ollie)** married **Marcellus Neal Vinson**, son of **Elisha** and **Lucy Jones Vinson**, my other namesake, but from a different line of **Jones**' out of South Carolina. Three children born to this union were: **Laura Bernice, Leland Morgan**, and **Elizabeth Estelle**, my mother.

Judge Aaron's 6th child, **Jettie Irene** died before reaching her 18th birthday.

Another of Judge Aaron's sisters, **Leonora (Nora)** never married. She taught school for a number of years. Also she ran a little country store and a small post office called Earnest. She stayed with and cared for her aging mother. She was very jolly and did lots of things for the sick in the community. In her later years she lived with her youngest sister, **Fannie**.

Frances Jane (Fannie) married **Thomas Browning**, member of the Browning family that was involved in beginning our church.. They had 2 children, **Nora Eula**, a beautiful girl who died in her teens and **Gemmie Bruce** who married **Daniel Porter Meadows**. **Cousin Gemmie** died right here at Hopewell while teaching Sunday School.

In 1880, **Judge Aaron** worked at the Lime Kiln as a guard for prisoners. The prison was on the same side of the road as the Kilns. His family lived in a house across the road. Near the house was a large commissary. All of the buildings were made of limestone. **Judge Aaron**'s daughter, **Louanna**, told this tale. Her mother sent her and her brother **Dorsey** to the commissary for supplies to be bought from tickets in a ticket book. On her way back home, she threw the balance of the tickets in the ticket book away. I don't have a record of what her punishment was, but she was punished...

My grandmother used to tell this story. When her parents lived at the Lime Kiln, the two oldest children wanted to go down to the commissary to play one night. Their father told them he had heard two old cats talking that day saying, "There is going to be a rowr, rowr, rowr rowr down there that night, so they better not go.

My grandmother, **Laura Olivia**, was born on April 16, 1884 at what was known as the Browning place near Hopewell. It was a large two story house with a long front porch. Believe it or not, some 54 years later, I was born in the same house! I wish I had taken a picture of the old house before it was destroyed, but another relative also born there made a stick replica and gave it to me.

Picture of front of replica of Browning house

Stick house picture

In 1889, **Judge Aaron** and **Laura Jane** bought a tract of land from **James Browning** near Hopewell Church and built a nice house of long leaf pine timber. **Laura Jane** did not live long enough to enjoy their new home. She died March 1, 1891. My grandmother was not yet seven years old. (Pictured below is the house about 1955.)

Story house near church

Pictured above is Judge Aaron and his second wife, Sultana Cadenhead and five of his children with his first wife. (To my knowledge, we have no pictures of his first wife.) This was made prior to the birth of their first child, about 1892. Children, back row, left to right Labon Morgan, Nettie Willa, Eugene Dorsey and front row, l to r, Jettie Irene, and Laura Olivia. Louanna Estelle had already married.

Judge Aaron's second marriage was to **Sultana Cadenhead**. They had 3 children. **Jessie** married **Ethel Deas**, **Alto** married **Will Morrison**, and **Otis** married **Lillie Thomas**. **Uncle Jessie** built this pulpit, altar and altar rail here at the church. **Alto** died young, but I remember **Aunt Will** and their son, **Charles,** with fond memories. **Charles** used to come visit Grandma and Papa in the summer. He loved buttermilk. I tried to drink it to be like him, but I could never acquire a taste for it. He called me "Lucy Bug". I was called Lucy until I started to school and told my teachers I wanted to be called Annette. **Uncle Otis** and **Aunt Lillie** were faithful members and practiced good stewardship. I used to love to visit their old large farm home and also like going to their "town" general store.

Toward the end of his life **Judge Aaron** became a licensed Methodist Protestant minister. In 1900, **Judge Aaron** and **Sultana Cadenhead**, his 2nd wife, deeded land to the Hopewell Church for the building and the cemetery, and for this we all can be grateful. I counted 12 **Jones**', 12 **Lynches**, and 15 **Storys** buried here in this cemetery, not to mention the **Allens, Brownings, Riddles, Thomases, Howards, Martins, Meadows', Vinson's, Hanners', Hoople's, Porch's** and others, from which we descended. **Judge Aaron** died in 1922, but **Sultana** lived until 1953. I know that my grandparents, **Dock** and **Ollie Vinson**, lived with her for several years until 1941, but I do not know when they moved in with her or who stayed with her after they moved out. My brother and I both remember the fig tree just outside the back door, climbing in it and enjoying the fruit. **Hartwell** thinks a family of Riddles moved in to stay with her, but I do not remember that.

This is a picture of Grandma Sultana Story (seated) with two of her children and three of her step children. Left to right: Louanna Story Crawford, Laura Olivia (Ollie) Story Vinson, Dorsey Story, Otis Story and Jesse Story.

Some 1903- 1924 Records

(oldest available)

The first page of the oldest membership record found was a list of people on probation in 1903. I am not quite sure what this meant, but apparently, a person had to be approved before being given membership in the early Methodist Protestant Church. At any rate, the list consisted of twenty three names. Some of the names do, in fact, appear later in the rolls.

The membership pages were separated by gender. There were 63 men and 90 women on the rolls in 1903. In 1924, there were 57 men and 88 women.

Names on the 1903 male rolls include: Jones, Lynch, Story, McConnell, Butler, Littleton, Waldrop, Browning, Brown, Howard, Jackson, Burdell, Herring, Lenard, Martin, Ramsey, Duran, Freeman, Pickard, Gunter, Cawley, Shaw, Letlow, Crawford, Lyle, Massey, Chappell, Vinson, and Deslin,

Names of the 1903 female rolls include: Story, Jones. Lynch, Howard, Martin, Waldrop, Brigens, Browning, Word, McConnell, Crofard, Stripling, Brown, Whatley, Birens, Burdell, Littleton, Johnson, Riddle, Freeman, Gunter, Butler, Hunt, Durham, Byrd, Howell, Duncan, Foster, Ramsey, Walker, Herring, Blalock, Corley, Letlow, Liles, Harrison, Massey, Cawley, Cooley, Vinson, Bankston, Long, Herring, Phillips, Parker, Belrin, and Chappell.

In 1924, male names included: Browning, Lynch, Jones, Littleton, Herring, Ramsey, Cawley, McConnell, Foster, Vinson, Riddle, Story, Howard, Allen, Cooley, Riddle, Chadwick, Winslett, and Lisle.

In 1924, female names listed were: Foster, Jones, Story, Allen, Whatley, Word, Howard, Littleton, Butler, Durham, Ramsey, Herring, Blaylock, Cooley, Cawley, Riddle, McConnell, Freeman, Meadows, Vinson, Royals, Thomas, Bankston, Lynch, Johnson, Plott, Rudd, McKendre, Prather, Hanners, Grayham, Rice, Hinson, Piper, Lisle, and Broadwaters.

I hope I will be forgiven if I have not gotten the names right. The spelling of some of the names was questionable in my mind.

Hopewell Church Pastors

1846-2017

1846	First recorded Conference of the Alabama Methodist Protestant Church, Mt. Jefferson - to be supplied
1851	Rev. D.A. Ferguson
1852	Russell County Circuit started
1853-1858	No records available
1859	Delegate S.G. Hopkins
1860-1874	No records available
1875	W.H. Lynch
1876	(Lee Circuit Organized, 5 churches, Hopewell, Pierce chapel Morris Chapel, Pine Grove and Beulah)
1878	Rev. John Whittaker
1880	Rev. A.H. Ledbetter
1883	Rev. W.G. Frazier
1884	Rev. George Brewer
1885	Rev. J.A. Spence
1886	Rev. Cox and Rev. Sellars
1887	Rev. W.J. Nolen
1890	Rev. T.J. Ledbetter
1890-1910	J.A. Story, Lay Preacher, Goat Rock Church M.P.
1891	Rev. Jesse P. Morgan
1893	Rev. T.M. McGraw
1895	Rev. F.A. Gibson

	Delegate – Mr. Stanfield
1896	Rev. J.E. Chapman (3rd sub-district)
1900	Rev. John L. Mosley (licensed W.A. Lynch)
1901	Rev. S. H. "Kim" Lynch
1903	Rev. G.A. Gibson
1905	Rev. Finney Messer
1906	Rev. Charlie W. Walton
1908	Rev. A.C. Messer
1910	Rev. E.M. Bell
1912	Rev. J.J. Hardy
1914	Rev. J.E. Chapman
1916	Rev. W.D. Stewart
	(Revival by Rev. Kim Lynch – 1917)
1919	Rev. C.W. Walton
	(Revival by Rev. J.S. Eddins)
	(Revival by Rev. T.C. Cassidy)
1923	Rev. A.C. Messer
1924	Rev. Arthur Lynch
	(New church built 1925)
1926	Rev. W.C. Conner
1930	Rev. A.L. Lumpkin
1931	Alabama Conference in Antioch Church, Macon County
1934	Rev. E.A. Maddox
1936	Rev. Wilber Walton (5 years)
1939	Uniting Conference – Methodist Church
1942	Rev. T.H. Maxey
1943	Rev. Kelley Scott
1945	Rev. Robert Wilson
1948	Rev. H.F. Wesley
1950	Rev. Carl Williams
1951	Rev. Glenn Sirmon
1954	Rev. James Love
1955	Rev. Charles Pittman

(Lee Circuit changed, became a three church charge, Hopewell, Pierce Chapel and Morris Chapel)

1957	(Homecoming sermon by Rev. Glenn Sirmon)
1958	Rev. Gillis Crenshaw
1960	Rev. R.C. Warren
1963	Rev. Robert Hall and Rev. Sam Lowry
1964	Rev. Linwood Lewis
1965	Rev. Dick Cobb
1967	Rev. David Chunn
1968	Rev. Bobby Holliday
1968	(Became Hopewell United Methodist Church)
1971	Rev. C.D. Monday
1973	Rev. Robert Warren
1977	Rev. Tim Thompson
1978	Rev. Judd Stinson
1979	Rev. Phillip McVay
1983	Rev. Eugene Hall
1985	Rev. Andy Knight
1989	Rev. Andy Gartman
1993	Rev. Gene May
1995	Rev. Daniel Randall
2001	Rev. Russell Fulford
2003	Rev. Gloria Wilson
2005	Rev. Matt O'Reilly
2007	Rev. Davis Hollis
2008	Rev. Rev. Chris Walker
2011	Dr. Paul McCracken
2015	Rev. Drue Tubbs

Picture of church in 2017.

Printed in the United States
By Bookmasters